BARRON'

MW01328036

JOHN MILTON'S
Paradise Lost

BY

Ruth Mitchell

SERIES EDITOR

Michael Spring
Editor, *Literary Cavalcade*
Scholastic Inc.

BARRON'S

BARRON'S EDUCATIONAL SERIES, INC.
Woodbury, New York / London / Toronto / Sydney

ACKNOWLEDGMENTS

We would like to acknowledge the many painstaking hours of work Holly Hughes and Thomas F. Hirsch have devoted to making the *Book Notes* series a success.

All inquiries should be addressed to:
Barron's Educational Series, Inc.
113 Crossways Park Drive
Woodbury, New York 11797

Library of Congress Catalog Card No. 84-18423

International Standard Book No. 0-8120-3435-X

Library of Congress Cataloging in Publication Data
Mitchell, Ruth.
 John Milton's Paradise lost.

 (Barron's book notes)
 Bibliography: p.131
 Summary: A guide to reading "Paradise Lost" with a critical and appreciative mind. Includes background on the author's life and times, sample tests, term paper suggestions, and a reading list.
  1. Milton, John, 1608–1674. Paradise lost.
 [1. Milton, John, 1608–1674. Paradise lost. 2. English literature—History and criticism. I. Title. II. Series.
 PR3562.M53   1984   821'.4   84-18423
 ISBN 0-7641-9120-9

PRINTED IN THE UNITED STATES OF AMERICA

456   550   98765432

CONTENTS

ADVISORY BOARD

We wish to thank the following educators who helped us focus our *Book Notes* series to meet student needs and critiqued our manuscripts to provide quality materials.

Murray Bromberg, Principal
Wang High School of Queens, Holliswood, New York

Sandra Dunn, English Teacher
Hempstead High School, Hempstead, New York

Lawrence J. Epstein, Associate Professor of English
Suffolk County Community College, Selden, New York

Leonard Gardner, Lecturer, English Department
State University of New York at Stony Brook

Beverly A. Haley, Member, Advisory Committee
National Council of Teachers of English Student Guide Series, Fort Morgan, Colorado

Elaine C. Johnson, English Teacher
Tamalpais Union High School District
Mill Valley, California

Marvin J. LaHood, Professor of English
State University of New York College at Buffalo

Robert Lecker, Associate Professor of English
McGill University, Montréal, Québec, Canada

David E. Manly, Professor of Educational Studies
State University of New York College at Geneseo

Bruce Miller, Associate Professor of Education
State University of New York at Buffalo

Frank O'Hare, Professor of English
Ohio State University, Columbus, Ohio

Faith Z. Schullstrom, Member, Executive Committee
National Council of Teachers of English
Director of Curriculum and Instruction
Guilderland Central School District, New York

Mattie C. Williams, Director, Bureau of Language Arts
Chicago Public Schools, Chicago, Illinois

HOW TO USE THIS BOOK

You have to know how to approach literature in order to get the most out of it. This *Barron's Book Notes* volume follows a plan based on methods used by some of the best students to read a work of literature.

Begin with the guide's section on the author's life and times. As you read, try to form a clear picture of the author's personality, circumstances, and motives for writing the work. This background usually will make it easier for you to hear the author's tone of voice, and follow where the author is heading.

Then go over the rest of the introductory material—such sections as those on the plot, characters, setting, themes, and style of the work. Underline, or write down in your notebook, particular things to watch for, such as contrasts between characters and repeated literary devices. At this point, you may want to develop a system of symbols to use in marking your text as you read. (Of course, you should only mark up a book you own, not one that belongs to another person or a school.) Perhaps you will want to use a different letter for each character's name, a different number for each major theme of the book, a different color for each important symbol or literary device. Be prepared to mark up the pages of your book as you read. Put your marks in the margins so you can find them again easily.

Now comes the moment you've been waiting for—the time to start reading the work of literature. You may want to put aside your *Barron's Book Notes* volume until you've read the work all the way through. Or you may want to alternate, reading the *Book Notes* analysis of each section as soon as you have finished reading the corresponding part of the original. Before you move on, reread crucial passages you don't fully understand. (Don't take this guide's analysis for granted—make up your own mind as to what the work means.)

Once you've finished the whole work of literature, you may want to review it right away, so you can firm up your ideas about what it means. You may want to leaf through the book concentrating on passages you marked in reference to one character or one theme. This is also a good time to reread the *Book Notes* introductory material, which pulls together insights on specific topics.

When it comes time to prepare for a test or to write a paper, you'll already have formed ideas about the work. You'll be able to go back through it, refreshing your memory as to the author's exact words and perspective, so that you can support your opinions with evidence drawn straight from the work. Patterns will emerge, and ideas will fall into place; your essay question or term paper will almost write itself. Give yourself a dry run with one of the sample tests in the guide. These tests present both multiple-choice and essay questions. An accompanying section gives answers to the multiple-choice questions as well as suggestions for writing the essays. If you have to select a term paper topic, you may choose one from the list of suggestions in this book. This guide also provides you with a reading list, to help you when you start research for a term paper, and a selection of provocative comments by critics, to spark your thinking before you write.

THE AUTHOR AND HIS TIMES

Americans tend to forget that they weren't the first to have a revolution. The English had theirs more than 130 years before the Thirteen Colonies rebelled. The English revolution consisted of a bloody Civil War from 1642 to 1649, the beheading of King Charles I in January 1649, and ten years of Puritan republican rule; it ended finally with the restoration of the monarchy under King Charles II in 1660.

These events aren't merely the background to John Milton's life: they were his life. We usually think of the war as a conflict between the Cavaliers and the Roundheads. John Milton was a Roundhead. The Cavaliers, or Royalists, supported the king and tended toward Catholicism. They believed in an aristocracy that had the right to special privileges, both in politics and in religion. The Roundheads, or Puritans, believed in a wider distribution of political and economic power and the right of every man to enjoy direct access to God.

Milton was so strongly committed to the Puritan cause that he accepted a government position under Oliver Cromwell, who ruled as Lord Protector from 1649 to 1658. Milton was a radical Christian individualist who objected strongly and vocally to all kinds of organized religions which, he believed, put barriers between man and God.

Milton was therefore a rebel because he identified himself with a revolutionary cause. *Paradise Lost*, his masterpiece, is about rebellion and its consequences.

One way of looking at the poem is to see it as Milton's working out of his own position. Although many readers have thought that Milton is really Satan, he probably saw himself as Abdiel, the angel who refuses to go along with Satan. Milton was arrogant in his belief that he understood the truth and had a duty to explain it for everyone's good.

The revolution he lived through changed every aspect of English life. When he was born in 1608, Shakespeare was still alive and Queen Elizabeth was only five years dead. Her influence was still felt. She had been an absolute monarch who regarded Parliament as a necessary evil in order to get money for her projects. When Milton died in 1674, Charles II reigned as constitutional monarch without any real power except that granted to him by Parliament.

Milton's circumstances changed drastically during his life. His family was reasonably well-to-do. They lived in London, which was Milton's home for most of his life. His father was a scrivener, a sort of combined notary and banker, who was wealthy enough to afford private tutors for his son, then schooling at St. Paul's and Christ's College, Cambridge University. Perhaps just as important for Milton's development was the fact that his father was a musician and composer. One of the most attractive features of Milton's poetry is its marvelous musical qualities.

Since Milton had a small private income, he did not seek a profession when he left Cambridge, but stayed at home writing poetry and increasing his already amazing stock of knowledge. Some people have said that Milton was one of the most learned men England has ever known. He wrote poetry in Latin, Greek, and Italian, and read almost all the literature surviving from the Greek and Roman periods. He even read the Bible in Hebrew.

Just before the religious and political quarrels in England came to a head, Milton went abroad for fifteen months, meeting and talking with learned and famous men all over Europe. He met Galileo and looked through his telescope, a fact Milton mentions more than once in *Paradise Lost*.

When he returned, he put his learning and considerable rhetorical force at the service of the Puritan cause. He wrote a series of scorching political and religious pamphlets: he condemned bishops, not only the Catholic ones but those of the Protestant Church of England; defended the liberty of the press against censorship; even advocated divorce. Many of the controversies in which he engaged with heat and passion we find difficult to sympathize with now, but Milton championed them with vigor and made himself not only well known but also well hated.

The Civil War deeply affected his personal relations. His brother Christopher adhered to the Royalist side. Milton married into a Royalist family in 1642. He was swept off his feet by a fun-loving seventeen-year-old, Mary Powell, whose family was originally the source of Milton's private income (they had bought property from Milton's father). The Powells kept Mary away from Milton, in Oxford where King Charles I made his headquarters, and did not let her travel to London to live with her husband until 1645.

By that time Milton had been extremely vocal publicly on the subject of divorce (he even advocated polygamy at one time) and had had an affair with a Miss Davies. His was a lively household, for he looked after and educated his dead sister's three sons. (One of them became Milton's biographer and the source of most of what we know about Milton's life.) He took his duties as schoolmaster very seriously; the boys were beaten if they did not learn their Latin and Greek grammar. The civil disturbances flowed in and out of the house as Milton's pamphlets provoked angry opposition and his supporters cried for more.

Only six weeks after King Charles I's head rolled from his body (Milton's friend Marvell wrote a famous ode on the occasion), Milton became Latin secretary to Oliver Cromwell. It was his duty to compose all the government's diplomatic correspondence in Latin, a job probably concerned as much with public relations as with accurate translation.

By this time Milton was blind, probably as a result of a cyst or tumor of the pituitary gland. For the rest of his life he depended on others to read to him and to write at his dictation. Because he was not a patient man—he had the arrogance of a person conscious of his talents—reading and writing for him was not easy. His daughters objected to the tyranny he showed in demanding their time and then complaining when they read incorrectly.

Mary died in 1652, leaving a blind man with three young daughters, the eldest mentally retarded. Milton married again in 1657, but his second wife, whom he called in a famous sonnet his "espoused saint," lived only fifteen months and died after giving birth to a daughter, who also died. Milton married a third time, to a woman who looked after him for the rest of his life and managed to bring order to a household full of quarreling daughters, relatives, and visitors to the famous writer.

In 1658, Oliver Cromwell had died, leaving England in the incompetent hands of his son, Richard. The passions that had caused the Civil War had cooled, and the king's son was asked to return, but on

the conditions which brought about the English constitutional monarchy.

The coming of Charles II meant the end of Milton's
government job. For a time he was in danger of his life
and had to be hidden by friends—one of his pamphlets had argued strongly in defense of Charles I's
beheading. Milton retired from public life and devoted himself to the composition of *Paradise Lost*. By the
time he had finished dictating it to whoever got up
early in the morning, two other events had disturbed
Milton's never very tranquil life. In 1665 he was forced
by the Great Plague to leave London and live in a
Buckinghamshire village. A year later, in the Great
Fire in 1666, Milton lost the last piece of property he
owned. He lived the last few years of his life in considerable poverty, quite unlike the comfort of his first
pampered years in his father's house.

Paradise Lost (1667) is the culmination of his life's
work. His early poems, the exquisite "L'Allegro," "Il
Penseroso," "Lycidas," the masque *Comus,* and the
sonnets would all secure him a place among the finest
English poets. But it is *Paradise Lost* which makes it
impossible for you to ignore Milton. He wrote *Paradise
Regained* afterward, but it has nothing like the stature
of *Paradise Lost*. (It is not, as you might think, about
Christ's sacrifice, but about his three-day temptation
in the desert by Satan.) Milton's final work, *Samson
Agonistes,* is a Greek drama as impressive as *Paradise
Lost* in everything except size.

Milton died in 1674, just after the second edition of
Paradise Lost appeared. The poem was for that time a
modest best seller. It sold 1,300 copies in the first eigh-
teen months and earned Milton a total of ten pounds.
By the end of the seventeenth century, the book had

gone through six editions, including one published in 1678 with large engraved illustrations. It has never lost its status as a classic, and it has never stopped being a source of controversy. People love or hate *Paradise Lost*, for as many reasons as it has readers. The poem has retained its interest because it deals with subjects that will always concern us—good, evil, freedom, responsibility. And because, like any great work of literature, it's exciting to read.

THE POEM

The Plot

Paradise Lost follows the epic tradition in not telling the story chronologically, with one event following another in the sequence in which they occurred. Instead it begins at midpoint and tells the rest in flashbacks (and flash-forwards). Before we consider the plot as it actually unfolds in *Paradise Lost*, it is helpful to have in mind an outline of the story in chronological order.

THE CHRONOLOGICAL SEQUENCE OF EVENTS

God has three aspects, the Father, the Son, and the Holy Ghost or Holy Spirit. As creator, God the Father sets everything going, like a clock, so that he knows what is to happen but does not interfere with the running of it. In Heaven he is surrounded by angels ("angel" comes from a Greek word meaning "messenger"). When he decides to announce the equal status with himself of his Son, one-third of the angels rebel under the leadership of Lucifer, who becomes Satan, the Prince of Hell. A terrible three-day War in Heaven ends in the defeat of Satan by the Son, who drives all the rebel angels down to Hell, which God has created for them out of primal Chaos.

To replace the missing angels, God through his Son creates the World, and he puts Adam and Eve in the Garden of Paradise. Like the angels, they have free will. They live in pleasure, with frequent visits from the angels, but they must not touch two trees in the garden, the Tree of Knowledge and the Tree of Life.

Satan wants revenge on God for his defeat, so he tempts Eve to eat fruit from the Tree of Knowledge. She in turn tempts her husband, Adam. This is the original sin from which all mankind's troubles flow. The life of pleasure is over: man must work and woman must suffer childbirth pains. The two are driven from Paradise to make their home in the rest of the World, comforted by the knowledge that the Son will become man in a later generation and will die for their sins.

Now we turn to the plot as Milton relates it in *Paradise Lost*.

THE NARRATIVE SEQUENCE OF EVENTS

Satan has been in Hell for nine days, lying on a burning lake where he and his companions have been thrown by God and his angels. He moans to his companion Beelzebub about their terrible fate, but he resolves to continue his fight against God through other means.

He and Beelzebub raise themselves painfully from the lake and gather the fallen angels on the shore, where they build a great hall called Pandemonium. In it they hold a great council meeting about their next move.

One of the leaders counsels open war. Two others oppose the idea, saying they've had enough of God's fury and will make the best of it in Hell. Satan tells them of a rumor he had heard in Heaven that another kind of being was to be created. In order to find out how this creature could be corrupted for their purposes, he volunteers to go on a spying mission.

As he leaves, he meets Sin, who is his lover and daughter, and Death, his son and grandson, who guard the gate. They let him out into Chaos, the fundamental material of the universe from which God has fashioned Hell and the World.

Meanwhile in Heaven God foretells what is to happen and asks which of the angels will offer to die for man. The Son takes on the task and is praised for his sacrifice.

Satan alights on the top of the World (the universe, not the earth) and looks up into Heaven and down into the concentric spheres of the planets (see diagram, page 28). He flies down to the sun, where he asks directions of Uriel, the angel who guards the sun.

As Satan watches Adam and Eve in the Garden of Paradise, Uriel flies down to warn the angel Gabriel that Satan has deceived them both and is on earth. Satan overhears Adam telling Eve that they are forbidden to eat the fruit of the Tree of Knowledge. He conceals himself until night, when he becomes a toad and sits beside Eve's ear. Two guardian angels, Ithuriel and Zephon, find him and bring him to Gabriel. Gabriel threatens to drag Satan in chains to Hell if he's found in the garden again.

Eve tells Adam her terrible dream, induced by Satan. She dreamed that she ate the fruit and became a goddess flying above the earth. She is very frightened and needs Adam's comfort. When they go out to their daily chores in the garden, they find that the archangel Raphael has come to visit them.

In a very long flashback, Raphael tells Adam (Eve is sometimes there and sometimes doing her housework) what happened before he was created. He tells the story for a reason: he wants to warn Adam against

Satan, who, he feels sure, has some evil design in coming to earth.

Satan was originally called Lucifer and was one of the highest angels in the heavenly host. On the occasion of the Great Year, which comes every 36,000 years, God proclaims his Son equal to him. Lucifer's pride is so hurt that he draws away one-third of the angels with him into the North, where they prepare to fight a war against God. One of the number, Abdiel, is appalled at Satan's rebellion and refuses to be part of it. He runs back to the Mount of God, where he finds that the faithful angels already know about the rebellion and are preparing for war.

The War in Heaven lasts three days. On the first day, the rebel angels don't do well. They experience pain for the first time, although their wounds are never fatal because they are immortal. On the second day, they bring out cannons which they have built overnight and introduce gunpowder into Heaven. At first the heavenly host is bowled over, but they recover and throw hills and mountains as if they were snowballs.

On the third day God sends out his Son in his war chariot. It is soon over: the angels are driven over the edge of Heaven into Hell. That brings us back to the point where the poem began.

Raphael continues the story, telling Adam about God's creation of the earth. Adam reciprocates by telling Raphael about the making of Eve from his own rib and his great love for her. Raphael cautions him against worshipping her excessively and then leaves them in Paradise.

The next morning Eve suggests that they should work separately in order to get more gardening done. Adam reluctantly allows this, despite his misgivings. In the form of a serpent, Satan tempts Eve to eat fruit from the Tree of Knowledge, using the argument that he, a beast, received the gift of speech after eating it and God hasn't killed him. She finally eats the fruit and then persuades Adam to eat some as well. Because he loves her so much and does not want to be parted from her, he eats it.

The Fall has happened. Adam and Eve copulate like beasts and fall asleep like drunkards. When they awaken they realize for the first time that they are naked, and they begin to quarrel, furiously reproaching each other.

The universe reacts with groans to the dreadful event. God sends down the Son to judge Adam and Eve. Their happiness and immortality are taken from them. Adam must work and Eve must suffer the pain of childbirth, and both must die. The serpent will be punished by always being the enemy of man.

Satan begins his return journey in what he thinks is triumph. At the top of the World he meets Sin and Death, who have built a road leading from the gate of Hell to the World. Satan joyfully shows them their prey, waiting for them down on earth. He returns to Pandemonium, where the fallen angels are waiting for him in council. He announces his triumph, but they all immediately become snakes and the entire hall is filled with hissing. Although they eventually regain their shape, they must each year become snakes for a time to remind them that Satan became a snake to deceive man.

As Sin and Death move into their new quarters, drooling at the thought of feasts to come, God causes the angels to make the World as it is now—with extremes of weather, seasons, and bad planetary influences. Surveying the wreck of the beautiful World they have known, Adam and Eve throw themselves on God's mercy.

He responds to their prayers and the Son's pleas for them by agreeing that Death shall not strike them immediately, but they must leave the Garden of Paradise. Michael, the warrior archangel, is sent down to escort them out of Paradise into Eden and to leave a guard on the gate so that no one can enter.

But Michael gives them some comfort. He shows Adam what is to happen in the generations following, including Noah's flood, the descent into Egypt, the coming into the Promised Land, and the incarnation of God as Jesus Christ. Adam is greatly encouraged when he realizes that the great blessing of Christ and the gift of the Holy Spirit are possible for man only because of what he did. His sin is a "happy fault," since ultimately it will bring so much good to man.

Calmer but apprehensive, Adam and Eve leave the Garden of Paradise. As they walk away, they look back to see the fiery weapons of the angels guarding the gate. They look forward to their new life.

THE NARRATIVE STRUCTURE OF PARADISE LOST

The following schematic plan of the narrative structure of the poem makes it easy for you to see the distribution of the events. Note that the poem is divided into 12 books.

I.	Hell. Satan rallies the fallen angels
II.	Hell. The council in Pandemonium
III.	Heaven. The council in Heaven
	Limbo and the Sun. Satan's journey
IV.	Paradise. Satan spies on Adam and Eve
V.	Paradise. Raphael arrives
	Flashback: War in Heaven
VI.	Flashback: War in Heaven
VII.	Flashback: Creation of the world

The Characters

The characterization of *Paradise Lost* is peculiar. Only two characters, Adam and Eve, are people. Even they are different from us because they have not been born in the conventional way and neither is a member of a family. We don't see them in relation to other people because there aren't any.

All the other characters are immortal and have powers beyond our human understanding. But to describe them Milton must use human terms. That works to the advantage of some and the disadvantage of others.

Satan

Is Satan the hero or the villain of *Paradise Lost?* That's the question that has intrigued readers since the poem first appeared. It's too easy to say that Milton intended him for a villain but he turned out a hero. More probably Satan gets the benefit of the fact that Milton has to use human terms to describe him. It is easier—sad to say—to make absolute evil understandable than to do the same for absolute good.

Satan is an endlessly intriguing character. You will not be able to make up your mind about him even after you've read the poem and written essays on him. You will find yourself using him to characterize people you know about: "He's a bit like Satan in *Paradise Lost*—unbelievably talented but throwing it all away because he won't accept authority." Such people are fascinating and attractive, but they're infuriating when they waste it all for what they think is freedom.

All the main characters in *Paradise Lost* are concerned with freedom. Those who understand true freedom know that it consists of obeying God's will without question. (Abdiel is the best example—look at the discussion of his character further on.) Those who do not understand it think freedom means being free from someone else's will and following your own. Satan is chief among them. He is so offended by God's announcement of the Son's equality with him that he wants to be free of what he calls "tyranny."

Satan's essential characteristic is deception. He deceives himself, he deceives others. To trick the angel of the sun, Uriel, he changes shape to become a polite young cherub eager to see God's creation. When he approaches Adam and Eve, he changes into whatever animal will get him close to them. He becomes a toad to squat by Eve's ear and give her a nightmare. And of course he deceives Eve in the shape of a serpent.

His seduction of Eve is a masterpiece of persuasion. He knows exactly which buttons to push—her vulnerability to flattery, her desire for power, her susceptibility to a logical argument. Milton tells us that he summons up all the orator's art for this final push: his speech is certainly a textbook model. To his talents as leader and inventor, we can add the deception and polish of a Madison Avenue advertising man.

When we last see Satan he has become the serpent whose shape he borrowed to seduce Eve. There is little sense that he understands the punishment he will eventually receive. He thinks he has won.

> I am to bruise his heel;
> His seed, when is not set, shall bruise my head:
> A world who would not purchase with a bruise,
> Or much more grievous pain?
>
> (X, 498–501)

Has Satan won his fight against God? Or is it just not in his character to understand his defeat?

Beelzebub

Beelzebub, whose name during the Middle Ages meant simply "devil," is Satan's second-in-command. He behaves like a foil for Satan, allowing his leader to demonstrate his best qualities. Beelzebub is quite content with his reflected glory.

Belial

Belial appears twice in *Paradise Lost*, once when he advises the angels not to fight again and a second time during the War in Heaven when he makes bad puns with Satan about the cannon.

Moloch

Moloch is the archetype of mindless force. He fought against Gabriel and was split in two, but since he is immortal he soon recovered. In the debate in Pandemonium he quite unreasonably counsels open war, without much sense of how victory can be attained in view of the recent devastating defeat. Where Belial is all charm and acquiescence, Moloch is blind and pointless defiance.

Mammon

Mammon is the engineer of Pandemonium, the miner who finds the ore for the golden building. He is "the least erected spirit that fell" *(I, 679)*, because his mind is on money.

Other Devils

Nisroc has a single speech, urging the rebel angels on the first night of the War in Heaven to do something quickly because he can't stand pain. *Mulciber* has no speeches. He is the architect of Pandemonium. Many other devils are named as they slowly move from the burning lake to the shore for the military parade. They are all false gods, those who seduced the Israelites away from God in the Old Testament, or the classical gods of Egypt, Greece, and Rome.

The Trinity

Christianity is based on a mystic trinity, a three-in-one, one-in-three godhead, God the Father, God the Son, and God the Holy Ghost or Holy Spirit. All three have existed since the beginning of time, but the Son is only revealed at the celebration of the Great Year, and the Holy Spirit does not appear in *Paradise Lost* at all except in a flash-forward to the time after the Ascension of Christ when the Spirit is sent as a comforter to man. When speaking of *Paradise Lost*, by "God" we generally mean God the Father, and "the Son" means God the Son.

God

Like Satan, God is a problem for readers of *Paradise Lost*. We like Satan too much and God not enough. People have suggested that in each case their charac-

ters are already given: we know God is good and we
know Satan is bad, so neither has to be shown in
action doing what is expected of him. But the truth
remains that we'd rather have Satan's company than
God's.

He elevates the Son without preparing the angels
for the news, and indeed without any obvious reason,
but that's his privilege. The rest of the universe must
adapt to him, not he to it.

He loses more than one-third of the angels to Satan.
One critic has said a loss of that size would make one
question God's management style. And there is a certain teasing quality to his actions: if he could so easily
order the fallen angels to be pushed out of Heaven,
why did he let the war go on for three days? It seems
capricious.

But he has virtues: he is a just and merciful judge.
He listens to the Son's prayers for Adam and Eve and
does not kill them, even though that was the punishment for eating fruit from the Tree of Knowledge. He
does everything he can to warn Adam and Eve, send-
ing them Gabriel to guard them and Raphael to
explain their danger to them. And he is deeply proud
of the Son and what he represents, love of man.

The Son

As a character, the Son has an important function in
Paradise Lost as the exact opposite of Satan. He is put
into parallel situations to demonstrate right behavior
when Satan demonstrates what is wrong. In Book III,
when we first meet the Son, he willingly takes on the
job of dying for mankind:

> Behold me then, me for him, life for life,
> I offer, on me let thine anger fall;
> Account me man; I for his sake will leave
> Thy bosom . . .
>
> (III, 236–239)

Satan too has willingly taken on a courageous task, but he did it to destroy mankind, to complete his revenge on God. The Son always obeys God immediately, with a grace that shows his perfect freedom. He is the executive branch and God the legislative branch of the heavenly government. He can use the power of God, for example when he rides out in his chariot and pushes the rebel angels out of Heaven, but he doesn't abuse it.

His great characteristic is his special love for man. From the moment that he accepts his position as the future redeemer, he represents man's interests before God. When he judges Adam and Eve after the Fall, he does so as "both judge and savior sent," and immediately after pronouncing judgment he begins to look after them. He gives them clothes made of the skins of beasts and shields them from God's sight.

In the flash-forward in Book XII, we see the culmination of the Son's devotion to man, when he is born, lives, and dies for man. To him God gives the privilege of cleaning out Hell on the day of judgment, when a new Heaven and a new earth are created.

The Son is not blandly acquiescent. He knows that the sacrifice he will make for man is going to be painful beyond belief. He is quite capable of reminding God that the force of man's fall will be felt by him— "worst on me must light." The Son has dignity without coldness and obedience without fawning. It is a great deal easier to like him than God, for his function in the Trinity is to be man's side of God.

Raphael

Raphael is the archangel who spends the most time with Adam and Eve and therefore with us. He comes down in Book V and doesn't return to Heaven until the end of Book VIII. He is a magnificent figure with six pairs of wings which drape around him like a many-colored robe. He walks in great dignity to meet Adam and then acts as a gracious guest, obviously enjoying the food and complimenting Eve on it.

Raphael is a great teacher and storyteller. He explains everything that Adam wants to know— sometimes a little more than we want to know. Through his eyes we see the War in Heaven and the creation.

Michael

Michael is the warrior archangel. He leads the heavenly forces in the War in Heaven, with Gabriel as his second-in-command. It is Michael who engages in single combat with Satan, challenging him first in a speech where he threatens to send him to Hell. In their battle, which is like a conflict between two planets in its enormous scope, Michael wounds Satan with his great two-handed sword. It brings the fight to an end, but Satan soon recovers.

God chooses Michael to carry out the judgment that Adam and Eve must leave the Garden of Paradise. Adam understands the significance of the choice as soon as he sees him: Michael is armed, dressed in military splendor. He has come to carry out a sentence, although with grace and mercy.

Gabriel

Gabriel has the somewhat thankless job of guarding Paradise. It is thankless because Satan slips by Gabriel and the guards twice. After the first occasion, when Gabriel, Ithuriel, and Zephon confront Satan, Gabriel is willing to fight him, but God forbids with a sign in the sky.

Uriel

Uriel is the angel who guards the sun. Satan deceives him in the form of a little cherub asking his way to the new creation, earth. Despite the fact that

Uriel is one of the seven angels closest to the throne of God and is known to have sharper sight than any other angel, he cannot perceive the deception. This is not a defect of character but a theological condition. Only God can see through hypocrisy—neither men nor angels have that power. Uriel speaks with warm encouragement to the young apprentice angel.

Abdiel

This is the character Milton identified with. Abdiel is a rebel against rebels, the one angel who realizes before it is too late that Satan's cause is wrong. His name means "servant of God," and that he proves himself to be.

He stands in the middle of the rebel angels and tells Satan he is wrong. Satan does not understand true freedom—the service of God who made him—but calls it tyranny. Abdiel will not hear God blasphemed (a religious term meaning "insulted"). His impassioned speech shows a clear understanding of a correct relationship to God. It makes us wonder why he came to be among the one-third of the angels who followed Satan to his headquarters in the North.

He receives the praise he deserves from God:

> Well done, thou hast fought
> The better fight, who single has maintained
> Against revolted multitudes the cause
> Of truth, in word mightier than they in arms
> *(VI, 29–32)*

The praise from God and his own conviction of right make Abdiel bold enough to challenge Satan on the first day of the war. He steps out from the army and addresses Satan as a "fool." Satan attempts to mock him and the others by calling them lazy: they'd rather take the easier path of serving God with "feast and song" instead of seeking their freedom.

Abdiel's last speech is the best exposition of "true freedom" in the poem: it is freedom to serve the highest, as God and nature both command. It is not freedom to seek to exercise your own will, but servitude to yourself. Satan is welcome to reign in Hell; Abdiel will serve "in Heaven God ever blest." And with that he strikes the first blow of the War in Heaven. It is his privilege as the champion of truth.

Other Angels

Ithuriel finds Satan squatting next to Eve's ear while she sleeps. As he touches the toad with his spear, it immediately becomes Satan. A slanging match follows. *Zephon* accompanies Ithuriel on the mission, and together they bring back Satan to Gabriel. *Zophiel* is the cherub who sees the approach of the rebel army on the second day of the War in Heaven and warns the heavenly host.

Adam

The clue to Adam's character is his relationship to Eve. It ought to be his relationship to God, but it isn't—and that fact causes Adam's fall. Adam has to argue with God to get Eve (although it is only a mate he seeks at that point). When he sees her he falls so deeply in love with her that everything good seems embodied in her. He knows that Eve is not as close to God as he is, and he realizes that it is her beauty that he worships. Love is supreme and love "leads up to Heaven."

It is for love and for Eve that Adam eats the apple. As soon as he sees her with a branch from the Tree of Knowledge in her hand, he knows what has hap-

pened—as she does not. In his soliloquy, he makes
his decision:

> for with thee
> Certain my resolution is to die;
> How can I live without thee?

(IX, 906–908)

So his fall is different from Eve's. He does not directly
fall to temptation, but to his desire to be with her, no
matter what happens. God the Son puts his finger on
the matter right away: "Was she thy God, that thou
didst obey / Before his voice?" (X, 145–146). Adam has
upset the proper order of things. Nothing must come
before God.

He certainly learns from experience, although too
late. Before the Fall, he allows Eve to persuade him
that it is all right for her to work in the Garden separately from him—the fatal decision. But afterward he
accepts neither of her suggestions—that they not
have children and that they commit suicide.

Following his initial despair after the Fall, Adam's
character improves. He forgives Eve with the sensible
idea that they must now be each other's comfort in a
world changed from the Paradise to the kingdom of
Sin and Death. It is Adam who suggests that they
should plead for God's mercy. He asserts his leadership by insisting that Eve leave him alone to speak
with Michael. And it is to Adam alone—Eve sleeps
under a benign drug—Michael reveals the future.

Adam's relationship to the angels who visit him
from Heaven is always courteous and correct, for he
knows that he is inferior to them in the hierarchy
established by God. He has no difficulty with that
position. It seems as if Adam was made to be a fol-
lower rather than a leader until the Fall brought him
face to face with his responsibility.

Finally he has learned. His last speech, as Michael
points out, is "The sum / Of wisdom." In it Adam says

that it is best to love and fear God; to depend on him; to work against evil, content with small victories; to stand up for the sake of truth, no matter what it costs; and to die understanding Death is the gate to life.

This is very hard won wisdom. But Adam is the first man, and like all of us after him, he can only learn through bitter experience.

Eve

Looking at Eve through twentieth-century eyes, we find it difficult to separate her character from our feelings of indignation about the role she is given. Certainly Milton was sexist; he could not be otherwise given his times and his religion. He has to tell a story that was itself sexist, because it is a myth with a social purpose.

Poor Eve suffers from Milton's time and place. She is the "weaker," she was made not directly in God's image but from part of Adam's body, she must worship God through Adam, not in her own right. She is beautiful, yet her beauty is her downfall when the serpent flatters her, and it is downgraded in value by both Adam and Michael.

When left to herself she acts in no way that could be faulted. But it is Eve's ear, not Adam's, into which Satan pours the bad dream. And the effects of it cause her to argue with Adam that she should go separately to work in the garden. (There is no evidence that she had ever suggested this before the dream.) And of course it is Eve who is tempted by the serpent.

Her behavior during the first exchange with the serpent can't be blamed. This is the first time she has ever heard another creature speak except for Adam and those angelic but long-winded visitors. She listens with natural curiosity, but when they get to the tree, she says they might have spared themselves the

walk. There is no thought in her mind of doing anything forbidden.

What convinces her are Satan's arguments. They
are based on reason, and reason is a deceiver in Milton's theology. Right reason is the following of God's
law absolutely. False reason is man's own logic. To
trust to logic is to put your powers ahead of God's—
the fundamental error. We have to sympathize with
Eve in trusting her own reason. She's only human.

Her reactions after the Fall make that very clear. She
wants Adam to eat the fruit not for his own benefit
but for a self-serving reason: if she dies, Adam will get
another Eve. But she never says that to him. And she
puts the blame squarely on him for allowing her to
suffer temptation:

> Being as I am, why didst not thou the head
> Command me absolutely not to go?
> (IX, 1156–1157)

The quarrel is only too true to life.

Yet it is Eve who knows how to get out of the quarrel and on with the rest of their lives. She falls at
Adam's feet, even though he has repulsed her first
effort at reconciliation. Her submission wins him
over. Like Adam, she has become sadder, wiser, and
more mature after the Fall. She is very unhappy at
being forced to leave Paradise. It's a bit like a corporate
wife being told that she has to leave her home when
her husband is transferred. But just like the wife, Eve
realizes the truth of Michael's remark that her home is
wherever her husband is.

When Michael prepares to tell Adam the future history of mankind, his descendants, he puts Eve to
sleep with a drug. Yet when she wakes she knows all
that has been said and is comforted by the thought
that her "promised seed," the son of the Virgin Mary,
the "second Eve," will redeem mankind. This sym-

bolizes a different way of knowing—woman's intuition, direct instinctive knowledge rather than explanation and reasoning. It is another sign that "women are different."

Eve's last words refer to her consciousness of guilt for "my wilful crime." You might think Eve gets a bum rap. At least reflect that we no longer think that she represents the truth about women.

Sin and Death

Sin and Death are not characters but allegorical figures. That means they do what their names say they do. Whenever you see them, try to translate what they are doing into its meaning. Sin was born from Lucifer's head at the moment of his rebellion; this means that Sin begins with rebellion against just authority. Death was born as a result of an incestuous relationship between Sin and Satan; the meaning of this should be obvious.

Sin and Death keep the gates of Hell. When Sin opens the gate, it can never be shut again (another moral for us all). The mother and son together build the road from Hell to earth, so that while they are causing trouble with all the creatures there, the devils from Hell can easily travel to earth—and the condemned souls from earth will easily slide down to Hell. One of the horrible figures who keep running in and out of Sin's womb, Discord, begins to make food for her incestuous father Death as soon as they all get to earth.

We still use allegorical figures today. Our best-known one is Liberty, the statue in New York harbor. All her features, especially the lamp she carries, are meant to symbolize the freedom offered by this country.

Other Elements

SETTING

There is a built-in problem in talking about the setting of *Paradise Lost:* words we normally use, like "world," "universe," and "earth," have different meanings in the poem. Let's take a tour of the cosmos so that you can see the differences.

The largest frame of action is what we would call the universe—everything imaginable. Looking at it schematically, as in the diagram on p. 28, Heaven is at the top and Hell at the bottom. Both extend infinitely, Heaven upwards and Hell downwards. Between the two, filling all available space, is Chaos, which, like its name, is shapeless and confused. Chaos must have been the original stuff from which the other places were formed because Chaos (the name for the ruler as well as the place) complains that he has lost territory when God made Hell, and then lost more when God made a home for man.

Hanging in the center of the cosmos is what Milton calls "the World." We loosely understand by that word the earth on which we live, but Milton means what we call the universe. Milton's World is a sphere made up of ten concentric circles. The earth is at the center. Some of the circles revolving round it contain the planets (including the sun), the heavens, and a watery firmament.

The World (our universe) hangs from Heaven by a golden chain. At the top there is an opening, where three directions converge: standing at the opening (as

Satan does in Book III), you can look up the golden stairway to Heaven, down through the concentric circles to earth, and out into Chaos. When Sin and Death build their bridge across Chaos, they begin it at the Gate of Hell and end it at the opening to the World.

The earth for most of the poem does not look like anything we see now. The features that characterize it—seasons, weather, mountains, and valleys—are all brought into the world after the Fall. Angels are sent by God to turn the axis of the earth off dead center, thus introducing changes in climate and length of day. In Paradise, all kinds of animals and plants live together, without distinction of habitat. Flowers bloom constantly, and roses have no thorns.

Paradise is the name for the garden where Adam and Eve live. In the Bible, their home is called the Garden of Eden. Milton has interpreted this strictly. Paradise is the garden part of Eden. Eden is a land usually identified with Mesopotamia, the region between the rivers Tigris and Euphrates. But there is a tradition that Paradise was an island in the South seas, so Milton has it moved there during the flood.

The garden, Paradise, is watered by rivers that run under the boundaries (guarded by the angels) and come up as fountains. It is a real garden to the extent that it needs pruning and its fruits must be harvested, but there doesn't seem to be any weeding to be done and there is no mention of snails.

The important point to remember is that the entire setting is imaginary. The familiar terms should not mislead you. You are looking not at a landscape, but into Milton's mind.

The Geography of *Paradise Lost*

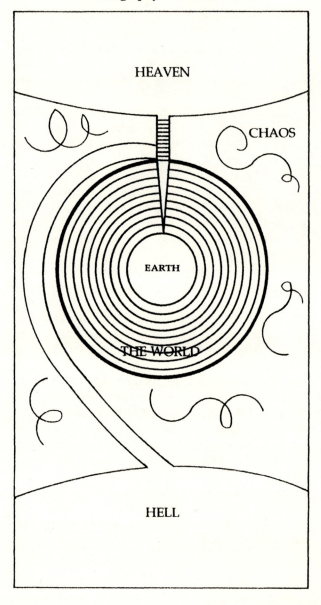

THEMES

Here is a list of the themes in *Paradise Lost*. They will all be studied more extensively in the discussion of the poem.

1. JUSTIFYING THE WAYS OF GOD TO MAN

The poem explains an entire theology. It is about the coming of sin into the world through the temptation of Adam and Eve by Satan after his defeat in Heaven. If Milton has justified the ways of God to man, all our questions about our relationship to God should be answered by implication from the poem. The success of the explanation of course depends on whether you accept the Christian world view—even whether you accept Milton's special brand of Christian individualism. The task of explaining an entire physical and moral system is not one we attempt today. We divide our systems, believing that the world is too complex for a single theory to explain.

2. GOD'S OMNIPOTENCE, OMNISCIENCE, AND FREE WILL

The poem insists that all events are brought about by choice. Satan chooses to rebel, Adam and Eve choose to eat the apple, knowing the consequences. Every man and angel has free will. At the same time, God knows everything that is to happen. But his foreknowledge has no effect on choice—the universe is like a clock God winds up and sets going: each of its parts performs without interference from God.

You will keep puzzling over this explanation throughout the poem. It sometimes seems that God is callous about his creation because if he is omnipotent, why doesn't he stop evil from happening? On the other hand, perhaps God does not have the power to

stop the clock or alter it once it's got going. In that
case, there must be something even more powerful
than God which programs him. It's an endlessly fascinating question. The poem will give you lots of
examples for a continuing argument.

3. INDIVIDUAL RESPONSIBILITY
Everyone makes his or her own decisions. That
means no one can blame anyone else for what happens. But there is a great deal of blaming in the story.
Only when people accept responsibility for their own
choices do they find peace within themselves and forgiveness and mercy from God.

4. THE NATURE OF FREEDOM
True freedom is total submission to God's will and
acceptance of what he wants in the world. It is freedom from self and self-will. Satan symbolizes the
wrong kind of freedom, rebellion against just authority. You are free when you understand where you fit
in relationship to God and in the hierarchy of
nature.

5. REASON
The highest exercise of man's reason is to understand and love God—and to trust him. This means
accepting what may seem illogical to human reason. It
also means not trusting human reason. Human reason may deceive because it is limited and cannot necessarily penetrate God's purposes, which are beyond
logic. It was perfectly reasonable for Eve to conclude
that she would not die because the serpent had not
died when he ate fruit from the Tree of Knowledge.
But she was trusting fallible human reason. She ought
to have gone beyond the logical argument and trusted
true reason—God's word.

6. THE HIERARCHICAL ARRANGEMENT OF THE UNIVERSE

Everything is arranged in an order, beginning with God at the highest point of all, going down through the angels to man, and from man down to beasts and plants. Each part of the hierarchy has its own order: in Heaven, the angels are lower than God and must take their orders from him. On earth, Adam is closer to God than Eve, and she must take her orders from him. The poem is about the violation of the order, first by Satan, then by Eve, and then by Adam, who puts Eve ahead of God.

7. HISTORY HAS A PURPOSE AND AN END

Although devastating in its results, the Fall is only part of a historical process. Adam's fall leads through many generations to the incarnation of God the Son as Jesus Christ. His fall is therefore a "happy fault" ("felix culpa") because it leads to the fulfillment of God's purpose. When Christ dies for man, he begins the process of redemption which eventually leads to the Last Judgment and the Second Coming. This will be the end of history, for then there will be a new Heaven and a new earth.

SOURCES

The sources of *Paradise Lost* are Milton's voluminous reading. The story of Adam and Eve and the temptation comes from the first few chapters of the Book of Genesis.

The story of the War in Heaven does not occur in one single place. References to it occur in the Book of Revelation, the last book in the New Testament. Oth-

er places where hints of a great war and of Hell are to
be found include the Book of Isaiah in the Old Testament and what are called the apocryphal books of the
Old Testament. Milton also adds some details from
the Book of Ezekiel, also in the Old Testament.

The vast majority of the allusions and references are
to the Bible and to the Greek and Latin classics. There
are also references to Arthurian legend, Italian epics,
and earlier English literature, especially the work of
Spenser, the author of the moral epic *The Faerie
Queene*.

STYLE: THE POETIC METER

The meter of *Paradise Lost* is iambic pentameter, the
meter in which Shakespeare wrote his plays. It is
often called "blank verse" because it doesn't rhyme.
Each line consists of five heavy stresses and five
minor stresses. In theory a line should read like
this:

da-dum, da-dum, da-dum, da-dum, da-dum

It happens to be the almost natural rhythm of the
English language, which is why it is easy to read blank
verse when you forget your fear of poetry.

Very few lines are strictly regular in the meter. Even
the famous first line reverses the stress in at least two
places, where *da-dum* is replaced by *dum-da* and *dum-
dum*. It also has one more syllable than the ten pre-
scribed by theory.

English poetic meter is not the simple matter of
counting feet that is often taught. It is a very complex
interaction of stress, length, and quality of sound. It is
better to forget the complications and read the poetry
as naturally as possible. You will then be able to

appreciate how Milton varies his rhythm and the musical quality of the words to fit what he wants to say. Read it out loud whenever you can, especially in the places where the speeches alternate like those in a play.

NOTE: How to Quote Poetry When Writing a Paper
Although you can ignore the line endings when you read the verse (and you should do so to make the reading move faster), please don't do that when you quote in an essay or paper. For quotations of two lines or less, you may run the quotation along within your paragraph, but then you must use quotation marks and slash marks to indicate where one line ends and the next begins: "Of man's first disobedience and the fruit / Of that forbidden tree . . . ," for example.

When you are quoting three lines or more, put them separately from your own writing. Don't use quotation marks, and copy the lines exactly as you see them on the page:

> Of Man's first disobedience and the fruit
> Of that forbidden tree, whose mortal taste
> Brought death into the world and all our woe.
> With loss of Eden . . .

If you need to indicate where the quotation comes from, use the Roman numeral for the number of the book and Arabic numbers for the lines. Put all this into parentheses, and place it after the final punctuation. For example, the last line of the quotation above would look like this:

> With loss of Eden . . .
>
> *(I, 1–4)*

The Story

BOOK I

The first book (1) introduces the theme of the entire poem, (2) introduces us to Satan and the fallen angels, and (3) tells us that we are reading an epic poem. In order to put himself in the epic tradition of *The Odyssey* and *The Aeneid*, Milton uses devices like the invocation, epic similes, and catalogs. They'll be explained as we come to them. They are used heavily in the first two books to establish the credentials of *Paradise Lost* as an epic, then they occur less often in the later books.

This book begins, as they all do, with Milton's prose summary, "The Argument." He is using the word in the sense of "subject matter," not as we do meaning a verbal clash. You will see "argument" used again with this meaning in line 24. The prose summary tells you the story, so you can use it as reference.

In Book I we meet one of the story's main characters, Satan. Whether he is the hero or the villain is one of the questions you'll face continually in *Paradise Lost*. It is obvious from this first book that Satan has qualities we all admire. He is a fearless leader, eloquent, inspiring, resourceful, even sympathetic to his followers' sufferings. Is he portrayed with these virtues because Milton wants to show us how we can be deceived by heroism? Have you found yourself attracted to "friends" who weren't good for you?

It is (unfortunately!) easy to identify with Satan when we first meet him in the imaginary landscape of Hell. We have all felt angry, bitter, and vengeful after a brush with authority. Perhaps you've received an F in a class where you thought you would pass, or gotten a speeding ticket when you were sure you weren't observed. These are small-scale personal grievances, but your feelings are intense. Satan's grievances result from conflict with God and have universal consequences. He wants to strike back at God for throwing him into a stinking pit of darkness, and he's going to do it by dragging us all down there with him.

Lines 1–25. The Invocation

Epics traditionally begin with a call for divine help in the task the poet has set for himself. Classical epic poets usually asked for the help of the Muses, the daughters of Zeus who watched over the arts. But Milton's muse is "Heavenly," Urania, who inspired Moses, the author of the Biblical Book of Genesis.

Milton wants to remind us that *Paradise Lost* is not only an epic, it is a Christian epic, and therefore—in his eyes—superior to its heathen predecessors. Milton wants to "soar above the Aonian Mount," that is, to exceed the accomplishment of the classical Muses. He will do this because of his "great Argument," his subject, which is nothing less ambitious than explaining the ways of God to men. Keep asking yourself whether Milton manages to do so. If he doesn't succeed, what has he explained?

Lines 25–83. The Scene in Hell

The Holy Spirit is asked to begin the story by naming the cause of mankind's fall. That of course is Satan, the first character we meet. Milton has told us in the Argument that the poem "hastes into the midst of things," because this too is a classical storytelling

device. We begin with Satan in Hell nine days after he
lost the War in Heaven, which would be just about
the midpoint of the story if it were told chronologically. We shall go forward in time to follow Satan's
revenge and backward to hear how and why he
rebelled and fought against God.

This kind of storytelling is quite familiar to us from
flashbacks in movies, plays, and TV drama. In fact,
the first book of *Paradise Lost* is the dramatic hook
which gets you interested, so that you will want to
find out what happened and why. In the flickering
flames of a burning lake (a contradiction which symbolizes the chaos of Hell) we barely see Satan as he
slowly becomes conscious of what has happened to
him and how far he is now from Heaven, where he
had hoped to reign.

He is accompanied by a vast number of followers,
one-third of all the angels in Heaven. Next to him is
Beelzebub, his trusted second-in-command. Beelzebub hasn't got the same fire for revenge as Satan. He
expresses the despair which you might expect from a
defeated angel who has been banished forever from
Heaven. Nevertheless he is always loyal to Satan and
accepts his leadership without question.

Lines 84–191. Satan and Beelzebub

Satan's defiance and his desire for revenge over-
come his pain. At first he seems dismayed as he
addresses Beelzebub, once like him among the bright-
est angels and now "O how fallen!" But as soon as he
speaks of God, "He with his thunder," Satan's rage
overtakes his sympathy. He will not repent or change.
"All is not lost" while he has his "unconquerable will /
And courage never to submit or yield." He will con-

tinue the war, either by force or by guile. Because we know the story of Adam and Eve and how Satan will corrupt them, "guile" is like a wink at a knowing audience.

You may think that Beelzebub takes a more realistic view of the fallen angels' terrible situation because he thinks further rebellion is futile. He regrets what has happened. The fallen angels may feel their strength undiminished, but perhaps God has left them that strength only so that they can work as slaves in Hell and has allowed them their immortality so that they can feel acutely their eternal punishment.

Satan is a good leader who knows when his subordinates need to be jerked out of what looks like self-pity. "To be weak is miserable" he declares, as he sets out a program of action: everything that God does must be opposed, even if God tries to bring good out of evil:

> To do aught good never will be our task,
> But ever to do ill our sole delight.

Then he draws Beelzebub's attention to the fact that God has recalled his forces and left the fallen angels to suffer in Hell. Things now seem calm enough for them to leave the lake and hold a meeting of their troops on a "dreary plain," to plot their revenge strategy.

Lines 192–375. The Epic Similes

As Satan prepares to rise, Milton gives us the first physical description we have of the Archenemy. To do this, he makes use of another classical device, the epic simile.

NOTE: Epic Similes   A simile is a comparison of one thing or idea to another; an epic simile is an extended comparison, often taking up several lines, in which the epic poet elaborates so much that additional ideas are brought in. Epic similes often occur in clusters, as they do here. Satan is so big that his trunk covers "many a rood," a rood being about a quarter acre. He is as big as the Titans and Giants who rebelled against Jove (Zeus), the supreme god of classical mythology. But it isn't a simple comparison of size—like Satan, the Titans and Giants were rebels against authority.

Giants and Titans aren't enough to emphasize Satan's size; he's also like a whale. Again this isn't a simple statement. This whale, like Satan, is a deceiver, because he seems to be an island and attracts a lost sailor to anchor in his hide. We can imagine what happens when the whale goes down. This story would have been well known to Milton's first readers, who had been brought up on "bestiaries," descriptions of animals in terms of the moral lessons they provide for mankind.

As Satan raises his huge head, Milton explains that he can move because God grants him free will: "Left him at large to his own dark designs." This is an important theme throughout *Paradise Lost*. (In Book III, God explains the doctrine of free will in his first speech.) God created all beings capable of action—angels and men—with free will, so that they can choose what to do. However—and this is the difficult part for us to accept—God knows their choices in advance, as he knows everything. You will have to make up your mind as you read the poem whether you find this a plausible explanation.

What Milton explains here is that God could have made it impossible for Satan ever to lift his head from the burning lake's surface, but instead he allowed Satan to follow his own course of action. Because Satan chooses to continue the battle through deceit, God has a chance to shower "infinite goodness, grace, and mercy" on man when Satan has ruined him.

Satan raises himself from the lake and with Beelzebub begins a flight to solid ground. The landscape of Hell looks like the devastation caused by an earthquake or volcanic eruption. More important than its physical appearance is Satan's reaction to the scene. He doesn't waste much time bemoaning the horrors of his kingdom. Hell may be miserable, but it is Satan's realm, where he is second to no one, not even God.

In any case, Hell and Heaven are mental states: "The mind is its own place, and in itself / Can make a Heaven of Hell, a Hell of Heaven." This is a familiar psychological truth. We all know someone who retains self-confidence and serenity in spite of failure and bad luck, while others are never happy despite all kinds of advantages.

Satan is beginning to emerge as a complex character. He has a rational understanding of his situation, for he certainly brought about his own Hell. He is apparently quite determined to think of it as his own personal Heaven. It's interesting to think about Satan as a reverse God, especially when you see him acting responsibly, as he does now, leading his unhappy followers to the shore. His physical stature is impressive: how do you feel about his moral qualities? Can evil have aspects of good?

Lines 376–520. The Catalog of Fallen Angels

For the listing of the fallen angels, Milton needs further help from his muse, the Holy Spirit. The listing is like a panoramic shot of the huge forces moving from lake to shore, with faces in the crowd picked out as Milton comments on them.

While dramatic, the list is also another device of classical epic. In *The Iliad* there is a famous catalog of ships, and in *The Aeneid* there are catalogs of the armies and their leaders who help Aeneas. These catalogs make the scale of the epic enormous: by naming everyone, the poet gives the impression that anybody who was anybody was there.

Don't try to follow every name in the catalog of fallen angels. To do so will only get you lost in a maze of Old Testament history. Instead, read parts of the catalog aloud to appreciate how impressive the names sound.

But you should know why the list is there. It shows that Milton had none of our multicultural appreciation for other religions or other mythologies beside the Christian one. In the later history of mankind, recorded in the Old Testament, the fallen angels become the false gods who turned the Israelites from the true God. The list includes the Egyptian gods and the gods of Greek and Roman mythology, "the Ionian gods" (*line 508*), who were also worshipped by people who

Milton thinks ought to have known better. For him, all other deities except the Christian God are companions of Satan.

Lines 522–669. Satan Reviews the Fallen Angels

Satan shows us again just how inspiring a leader he can be. He first "gently raised / Their fainting courage and dispelled their fears." Then he orders a military review with a brass band ("Sonorous metal blowing marital sounds") and a parade of all the divisions with their banners flying.

He proudly surveys the numberless army, by the side of which any other army would look like the pygmies fighting the cranes (*line 575*). A group of epic similes stresses the army's size: it is greater than the forces on both sides in the Trojan War, greater than any forces King Arthur or Charlemagne could command.

As he looks at the army (the similes have made it seem a cause for pride), Satan chokes with tears. His first few words express his affection and sympathy for his followers. How could such a "united force of gods" be defeated?

He soon talks himself out of weakness as he inspires his followers with hopes of regaining Heaven. They can't do it directly, since they obviously underestimated God's forces before. Instead he hints that a new world with beings equal to the angels is about to be created. There may be the chance to continue the fight through guerilla warfare.

The speech is so successful that the fallen angels flourish their swords and bang them against their shields as they hurl defiance at Heaven.

Lines 670–798. The Building of Pandemonium

NOTE: We use the word "pandemonium" to
mean any kind of confused, noisy gathering. Here we
see where the word comes from and what it really
means. It is a house for all devils, "pan" being the
Greek word for "all" and "demon" the Greek for
devil.

Summoned by heralds and trumpets, the enormous army surges toward Pandemonium, which has
been designed by Mulciber with materials mined by
Mammon, the god of gold. Milton reminds us that
angels are creatures with wings by using an epic simile that compares them to bees assembling outside
their hive. At a signal, they all shrink so that they can
fit into Pandemonium. They now look like pygmies or
the fairies that appear to drunken peasants on their
way home at night. The association suggests the
deceitful nature of the fallen angels.

But the leaders of the fallen angels do not shrink.
They are meeting privately in another part of Pandemonium to decide their strategy.

BOOK II

Lines 1–298. The Debate in Pandemonium

As suits his position, Satan presides over the debate
from a high throne, "that bad eminence." But the
debate is really a setup. Three fallen angels (later, the
gods who deceive the Israelites into worshipping
them instead of the true God) offer what you might
think are reasonable alternative strategies; but Beelze-

bub, like a well-trained staff officer, brings out the plan which we know will be agreed on, and then Satan takes on the job of carrying it out.

Moloch blusters that open war is preferable to remaining in Hell. We can't be worse off than we are, he says. If God wins again, we will be put out of our misery: God will "reduce / To nothing this essential, happier far / Than miserable to have eternal being." But it may be impossible even for God to annihilate them because they may be divine and therefore immortal *(lines 99–100)*. In that case, they already know the worst.

Belial is also unsure whether as fallen angels they are immortal, but he makes a different argument. If we can be annihilated, why take the chance? We might not be because God might not even give us that relief. And it is certainly better to have some "intellectual being / Those thoughts that wander through eternity" than nothing. War against God will not only risk annihilation, it will also hurt their chances of getting back into God's grace through good behavior *(lines 208–213)*.

Mammon's position is much less subtle than Belial's and more directly opposed to Moloch's. Instead of continuing to fight against God, let us make our kingdom here. There are plenty of resources, as Mammon knows because in Book I he mined the materials to build Pandemonium. Hell could eventually become a place rivaling the magnificence of Heaven; the torments they now feel will diminish with time.

Do you find any of these arguments convincing? It's obvious that Milton despises Belial, who "Counselled ignoble ease and peaceful sloth." This comment, addressed directly to us, may help us to under-

stand one of the reasons why Satan seems attractive—whether Milton intended him to or not. Satan is
active. He doesn't just accept his fate, he thinks of
ways to change it.

The other fallen angels like Moloch's idea best, fear-
ing another defeat. But it isn't what the leadership
wants.

Lines 299–505. Satan's Mission

Beelzebub, not approving of Mammon's speech or
the applause it receives, quickly dismisses its arguments. God is not going to let the fallen angels make a
home for themselves in Hell—he designed it as a
punishment, and it will never be otherwise. On the
other hand, open war is hopeless because God will
win again.

What about something easier? Beelzebub elaborates
the rumor of the creation of man, mentioned briefly
by Satan in Book I. These creatures are equal to
angels—perhaps they were intended to fill the gap
caused by the expulsion of the rebellious one-third—
but they will receive God's special favors. At least the
place should be investigated, in hopes of finding a
weak spot in God's armor, where he can be annoyed
if not defeated. Some trick may deliver the new creation into their hands, so that the inhabitants of earth
may join the fallen angels in Hell.

Satan puts the finishing touch on this managed
debate by praising their judgment in adopting the
plan he had in mind already. And then he raises the
essential question: who is going to be the spy?

Their cowardly silence gives Satan his chance. He
alone will take on the task of spying on God's new
creation. Such an assignment best fits a leader, who
should be prepared to take on any danger. A leader

can't accept the honors due his position without also accepting the hazards.

He stands up and ends the debate right there, knowing very well that some other fallen angel would try to claim the difficult job, thus detracting from Satan's glory. They all bow to him and praise him for his heroism, prompting an epic simile in which their harmony is compared to a beam of sun lighting up the evening sky after a storm.

Milton now adds his own comment: how shameful it is that devils can agree among themselves but men cannot *(lines 496–505)*. Milton had lived through a civil war and all the horrors of revenge when Charles II reestablished the monarchy. There were wars in Germany and France almost continually during his lifetime. If only mankind would unite against its common enemy, "hellish foes," and stop destroying each other! We can heartily agree, for things are no better three hundred years after *Paradise Lost*.

Lines 506–628. Life in Hell

The debate has broken up and its results have been proclaimed throughout Hell. The fallen angels are now free to go about their normal pursuits, while Satan prepares for his journey to the World.

The angels practice sports, race horses and chariots, and conduct military exercises, even tearing up the soil in their more strenuous efforts. Some are musicians, and they manage to produce songs so beautiful that they "Suspended Hell and took with ravishment / The thronged audience." Milton was a musician and his father a composer; music could never be evil to him.

One group of fallen angels acts like classical philosophers *(lines 555–569)*, arguing and disputing with eloquence about Providence, Foreknowledge, Will, and Fate—the subjects of *Paradise Lost* itself. But they are false philosophers who do not know the truth of the Christian religion. They can offer only solace and patience with their "pleasing sorcery."

Another group explores the rest of Hell. We are in classical territory here, and Milton exploits it fully. Both *The Odyssey* and *The Aeneid* include a visit to the underworld, where we find the same features—the four rivers of Hell, fire, ice, the torments of the damned, who suffer for their sins in life.

Lines 629–725. Sin and Death

Meanwhile Satan is off to the gates of Hell, through which he must pass before he can break through—literally erupt—into Chaos and then the World. An epic simile tells us that as he travels, he looks like a sailing ship so far away that it seems to be hanging in the clouds.

He soon reaches the nine gates of Hell—three brass, three iron, and three of the hardest known rock, adamant. All three gates burn continually but are never destroyed. They are guarded by two horrible creatures, one on each side of the gates: one is a woman, Sin, who is a serpent below the waist; the other is a man, Death, with no shape but blackness. He carries a dagger and seems to be wearing a crown.

NOTE: Allegory and Allegorical Figures   These figures have a different function in the poem than the characters we already know. Sin and Death are figures of *allegory*, which means that they represent in their appearance the parts they play in our lives. Sin is foul and misshapen, only half human, filthy with hybrid offspring who crawl in and out of her womb as they wish. She represents the unnatural confusion of sin, which distorts the proper order of things. Death is a black shadow, with a dagger to pierce his victims and a crown which symbolizes his rule over everyone. As we follow the interactions between Sin, Death, and Satan, you will be able to translate what they do into its meaning.

Death strides toward Satan, who stands his ground: he fears nothing in the universe except God and his Son. (When Satan looks Death in the eye, we are seeing allegory at work: Satan is immortal, and therefore he can defy Death.) He declares his intention to pass through the nine gates, but Death won't let him. As they stand ready to fight, Satan looks like a comet in the sky, and the threatening combatants look like the thunderclouds just before a storm. The fight never happens because Sin rushes between the two of them.

Lines 724–870. The Birth of Sin and Death

Sin prevents the fight by calling Satan "father"—as surprising to him as it is to us. She was born from Satan's head, just as in Greek mythology the goddess of wisdom, Athena, emerged from Zeus's head. But Sin came out of the left side of Satan's head. The left is connected with evil, and that's why we have the word "sinister," which simply leans "left."

She emerged precisely at the time Satan initiated the war against God. The meaning of the allegory is that Sin was born at the same moment as rebellion against God's authority.

Once born, Sin became Satan's concubine in a vile incestuous relationship. As Satan fell, she too was expelled from Heaven, but she was given the key to the Hell gates. While watching the gates, she gave birth to Death, a labor so difficult that it distorted her body into the shape of a serpent. Death immediately turned on his mother and raped her, causing the birth of monsters who continually torment her with their gnawing inside her body. She knows that Death would like to consume her but cannot do it.

So both Sin and Death are the offspring of Satan, an allegorical way of saying that Satan is responsible for the introduction of sin and death into the world, just as Milton said in the third line of Book I.

Wanting to be let out of the gates, Satan promises Sin and Death that he will take them back with him to earth after he has spied on it. Death smiles a ghastly smile as he thinks of more victims. Sin shows her nature by persuading herself that it is perfectly all right to disobey God, because her own father has asked her to unlock the gates. Sin can always find justification—as we know from our own experience.

Lines 871–1009. Chaos and Old Night

Sin opens the gates, which can never again be shut *(lines 883–884)*. The gates are wide enough to let an army, chariots and all, pass easily. They open on the realm of Chaos. Think of it as the first few moments after the Big Bang, when there is nothing but a soup of uncombined electrons and neutrons. Here "hot, cold, moist, and dry," the four elements in medieval science, contend in confusion. The prospect is so terrifying that even Satan pauses before launching himself out of the gates.

When he finally jumps into Chaos, he is swept first down and then up because the region is so chaotic that it is land, sea, and air, by turns and all at once. In three and a half lines composed almost entirely of monosyllables we get a vivid impression of confused and constant change:

> So eagerly the fiend
> Over bog, or steep, through the strait, rough,
>   dense, or rare,
> With head, hands, wings, or feet pursues his
>   way,
> And swims or sinks, or wades, or creeps, or
>   flies
>
>   (947–950)

After a prolonged struggle, he follows a "universal hubbub wild" to the place where King Chaos and his companion, Old Night, sit with their followers, who are all allegorical figures like Sin and Death. Note that Chance is one of these figures. Chance has no place in the ordered universe ruled by God—chance is chaotic by nature.

Satan asks Chaos and Old Night for directions to the World. He points out that if he reaches the earth and is successful in ruining it, Chaos will gain because he will have more territory. It is an argument Chaos is glad to hear; he grumbles that too much has been taken from him recently. He lost territory when God created Hell out of a corner of Chaos and then lost more when God created the World. It can be seen hanging on a golden chain from Heaven down into Chaos (see diagram, page 28). But the World isn't far away now, so Chaos wishes Satan luck. They have the same aims.

Lines 1010–1055. First Sight of the World

Satan plunges back into Chaos, again fighting his way through the confused elements. Milton tells us that later there will be a smooth road from Hell to earth, built by Sin and Death. It will follow Satan to the World and make a direct pathway for the devils to reach and corrupt man. You can easily see the allegorical meaning here.

As Satan comes to the edge of Chaos, day begins to dawn, causing Old Night to retreat so that his journey becomes easier. As he floats on the calmer air, Satan looks upward: there is Heaven, where he formerly lived, and hanging just below, the globe of the World.

NOTE: Milton's Cosmology   The World is not the earth, but the universe. In this imaginary cosmos of Milton's, we should forget our Copernican model of the universe. This is a schematic universe, where the component parts are placed in symbolic relationship to each other. Heaven is at the top, with unlimited extension upward. Hell, at the bottom, is Heaven's counterpart—it is unlimited downward. The space between is filled with Chaos. The World hangs suspended from Heaven, with a stairway leading down to an opening in the top of the sphere. Inside the sphere are ten concentric circles, with the earth in the middle. The sun and the planets revolve around the earth. The outside of the World is like a hard rind, which protects the World from the buffeting winds of Chaos.

Don't be too impatient with what may seem to you a ridiculous model of the cosmos. Milton knew about the Copernican universe (the archangel Raphael refers to it in Book VIII). Ask yourself why Milton might have wanted to retain the classical and medieval cosmology, with the earth at the center, for the purposes of his poem.

Reflect that science fiction also does not represent the universe as twentieth-century physicists and astronomers describe it. Think of those imaginary worlds where starships land to find robots. Like Milton, science fiction writers invent a background to fit what they want to say. They freely give planets atmospheres with or without important ingredients and put them in space at distances and in places where they need them for their plots. The important question for them and for Milton is whether the interactions which take place in these settings are believable and interesting to us.

BOOK III

The scene now shifts to Heaven, where for the first time we see God, his Son, and the angels. Book III is almost a point-for-point contrast with the two preceding books. All is light here, as all was darkness in Hell. In Heaven there is a council, as there was in Hell, but it is characterized by harmony and expressions of love. Just as Satan undertook the task of spying on man, so the Son takes on the burden of dying to redeem mankind.

Contrast this introduction to Heaven with Book I's description of Satan in Hell. You may find that God and his Son lack the characteristics—human failings—which make the fallen angels interesting. In Satan, God has a hard act to follow, and Milton hasn't given him much help. It's quite difficult to think of ways in which absolute authority could be given a

human face, especially when by definition God's
choices cannot be understood by man.

The poetry of the scenes in Heaven has a different
texture. There aren't many epic similes or classical
allusions in this book (which is one-third shorter than
Book II). Most of the classical references are found in
the first part, where Milton speaks of himself, and the
last, where Satan continues his journey and lands on
the sun. God and his Son converse in quite straight-
forward statements; whether you agree with God or
not, you can follow his argument quite easily.

NOTE: The Christian Trinity   In Christian theology, God has a mystic three-in-one, one-in-three unity.
The Godhead has three aspects: God the Father is the
original authority, while God the Son has a special
affinity for mankind, since he himself became man to
redeem Adam's sin. God the Holy Spirit is not mentioned until Book XII, when his coming is foretold.
But you will remember that Milton prayed to the Holy
Spirit after the first invocation.

The threefold nature of the Christian God separates
him from the Hebrew deity, who has only one aspect.
The Holy Trinity is a difficult concept to grasp, not
least because, although the Son and the Holy Spirit
are revealed later in time, they have existed as part of
God from the beginning. They are therefore present at
the creation of everything, including the angels.

Lines 1–55. The Invocation to Light

Milton went blind in his forties. He married his second and third wives without seeing them. The whole
of *Paradise Lost*—like *Paradise Regained* and *Samson
Agonistes*, the great works of Milton's maturity—was
dictated to secretaries and to his daughters, who did

not like the chore. Most of the poem was composed in the early hours of the morning, for Milton was an early riser. He waited impatiently for his secretary to arrive—like a cow waiting to be milked, he would say.

His anguish about his blindness is clearly expressed in the invocation to light. Book III is full of light, so he invokes its aid as God's first creation. But light cannot enter his eyes. Being blind does not prevent his enjoying classical poetry or the Hebrew Old Testament. Homer and other Greek poets were also blind. But the sense of regret is poignant:

> ever-enduring dark
> Surrounds me, from the cheerful ways of men
> Cut off, and for the Book of Knowledge fair
> Presented with a universal blank
> Of Nature's works to me expunged and razed,
> And wisdom at one entrance quite shut out.
> *(45–50)*

So light must shine inside his mind, communicating what is after all invisible to all men.

Lines 56–134. God's Explanation of Free Will

God the Father is seated on his throne in Heaven, with his Son by his side, looking down through the gate of Heaven, past the stairs, on Adam and Eve in Paradise and on Satan flying toward the suspended World. As he points out Satan to his Son, God describes what is going to happen: Satan will deceive Adam and Eve, who will listen to him and disobey God.

It is difficult to like what God says. He calls man ungrateful—"ingrate"—for his good fortune: "he had of me / All he could have." The contradiction between man's free will and God's omnipotence is easy to understand but hard to accept. God knows everything that is to happen and controls it all, but man is free. If he were not, then he could not choose and earn praise or blame.

NOTE: The Doctrine of Free Will   Free will isn't a dead issue. It's hotly debated in political science and philosophy classes. How free are you to do what you want? Are your actions under the control of your free will or is that your perception only? Milton thinks that man experiences his choices as free, even though God knows what the results will be. Because man does not know what God knows, man has the sense of complete freedom. Is it possible that this is a metaphorical way of describing our dependence on our context and heritage? We may not believe that God determines our actions, but a large part of them are controlled by genes, family history, economic circumstances, and environment—matters which, like God, are beyond our individual control.

God continues his explanation to the Son by saying: "Foreknowledge had no influence on their fault." Man is therefore responsible for his fall, but not as responsible as Satan and his followers. Because they fell "self-tempted, self-depraved," they will receive no mercy, but man will find grace and mercy, to God's glory.

Lines 135–415. The Heavenly Council
In contrast to the stench and darkness of Hell, Heaven is full of "ambrosial fragrance" and love shines on the face of the Son. He asks what God

intends to do with man: will Satan take the new creation down to Hell with him, or will God abolish it entirely?

God answers that he will offer mankind grace in the form of prayer, which he will hear gladly: "Mine ear shall not be slow, mine eye not shut." He will also give mankind a conscience to guide them.

But man will die eternally unless his mortal crime is atoned for by a heavenly being willing to die for him. Who in the heavenly host will become man and die a mortal death to redeem mankind?

There is the same silence in Heaven as there was in Hell when a parallel question was raised. Finally the Son offers himself as sacrifice. His faith in his Father is so strong that he knows God will not abandon him, but will allow him to kill Death himself: "Death his death's wound shall then receive." He predicts the glorious moment when he will return from cleaning out Hell to the "Joy entire" of God's presence.

The parallel between the Son and Satan will be drawn again, especially when we find out later what caused Satan's rebellion. Satan and the Son are two brothers—one good, one evil—fighting for their Father's attention.

God greets the Son's courageous offer with an outpouring of praise. The Son will become man in a virgin birth, mystically combining his nature as man (Adam's son) with his nature as God. Because the Son humbles himself to join mankind as one of them, he will unite in himself the qualities of man and God and become worthy to judge all creation. His sacrifice is so glorious that it will bring about "New heaven and earth, wherein the just shall dwell." God turns to the angels and commands them to worship the Son as his equal.

The angels sing a song which praises God in terms of light so radiant that even the angels must shade their eyes with their wings when they see it *(line 382)*. Then they sing praises to the Son, the warrior who defeated the rebel angels and now the redeemer who has "offered himself to die / For man's offence." The passage ends with the poet's vow to praise the Son endlessly as God's equal.

Lines 416–497. Satan in Limbo

Meanwhile, Satan lands on the outer rim of the World, suspended on its golden chain from Heaven (see diagram, page 28). He manages to find a spot where he is to some extent sheltered from the winds of Chaos, like a vulture who rests for a while on the windy plains of Mongolia, on his way to steal lambs for his prey. Notice how the epic simile makes a kind of double image: you see the ugly bird and Satan superimposed on one another, sharing the same characteristics.

There is nothing where Satan is walking up and down "alone bent on his prey." Later in the history of the World, Milton tells us, this place on the perimeter of the World will become Limbo. Here will be found the souls of those who are more misguided than sinful, who can't be sent to Hell but aren't good enough to enter Heaven. They will include the builders of the Tower of Babel and the Greek philosophers who wanted to become gods. Milton especially mentions those Roman Catholics who believed that putting on religious garments would get them into Heaven.

NOTE: Milton's Christian Individualism   England had become a Protestant nation in 1539, not for purely religious reasons but because King Henry VIII wanted to divorce his first wife and the Roman Catholic Church opposed divorce, as it still does. So Henry declared a Church of England, with himself as head.

The main difference between Roman Catholicism and Protestantism comes in the matter of access to God. The Roman Catholic Church believes in the need for intercession with God, through a priesthood specially trained to act as intermediary for the people. Protestants believe they can address God directly through prayer. Their clergy, who are permitted to marry, are counselors and advisors more than intercessors with God.

As Protestantism developed, groups arose believing that even the reduced priestly function of the Church of England was too much. The extreme is probably the Quakers, who have no priests at all. Milton was closest to being a Puritan, but his kind of Christianity is really unique to him. We can best describe him as a Christian individualist. He believed that he should obey only God and God's law, which was immediately obvious to anyone who believed with a pure heart. Milton had no use at all for the external shows of religion—even symbols like the cross.

Thus you can see why he despises Roman Catholic "Indulgences, Dispenses, Pardons, Bulls." All those who believed in them would be blown away from Heaven and whirled into Limbo, the Paradise of Fools.

Lines 498–629. Satan on the Sun

Leaving Limbo, Satan comes to the opening in the top of the World where he can look down into the concentric circles and up the stairs to Heaven. He stands in amazement looking down into the World, like a soldier on military reconnaissance who finds himself suddenly looking down on a new land or a magnificent city.

He throws himself down into the World and passes through the circle of the stars to land on the sun. The place is "beyond expression bright," brighter than jewels or the philosophers' stone which was said to turn any metal into gold. There are of course no shadows on the sun, so Satan easily sees an angel standing there with his back to him.

Lines 630–742. The Deception of the Angel Uriel

Satan is always daring and always deceitful. It seems no problem for him to change himself into a young angel or cherub with curling hair, gold-sprinkled wings, and a wand in his hand. He approaches the angel, who proves to be Uriel, one of the seven around God's throne, and addresses him.

Satan gives the flimsiest excuse for his presence: he has a great desire to see God's new creation, man, so much talked of in Heaven. Will Uriel kindly point out on which of the circling spheres Man is to be found?

Uriel suspects nothing. In fact, Milton tells us that only God can know the truth hidden by hypocrisy; not even angels can penetrate a lying appearance, especially when they are so good that suspicion is not part of their nature. Uriel praises the little cherub for his desire to see God's works and tells him with pride that he was present when the World was made. The globe down there at the center, the one half lit by the sun and half by the moon reflecting the sun's light, is earth. Uriel even points his finger directly at Paradise and tells Satan that he can't miss the way.

Satan bows respectfully, as a cherub would to a senior angel, and swoops down from the sun to the earth, landing on the top of Niphates, a mountain in the Armenian Taurus range.

BOOK IV

We find another change of scene and new characters in Book IV: the action takes place in Paradise. We meet not only Adam and Eve but the good angels who remained faithful to God and now guard Paradise. The action, which occupies an evening and night, moves dramatically from scenes in which Adam unwittingly tells Satan what he wants to know to a confrontation between Satan and his former companions; it also includes Adam and Eve's pleasure in their sexual union.

Lines 1–130. Satan's Remorse

The opening lines are a cry of regret: if only Adam and Eve had been warned now of what is about to happen! For Satan is on earth, looking at the Garden of Eden, of which Paradise is a part. Satan brings Hell with him wherever he goes—which you will easily understand in modern psychological terms as a continual state of tension and dissatisfaction: Satan is always full of revenge, remorse, and envy.

As he looks up at the sun, whose brilliance reminds him of his former glory in Heaven, he regrets his disobedience, for after all God's service is not hard. But ambition would always bring about his ruin because he would freely make the same choice. So nothing is left but Hell, for to repent would mean submitting to God. Not only would his pride prevent that, it also wouldn't last very long. The only hope is to divide possession of man with God, "more than half perhaps will reign."

Unknown to him, Uriel has been watching the little cherub who spoke so courteously to him. As the "cherub's" face contorts with anguish, Uriel realizes who he is.

Lines 131–287. Eden and Paradise.

Paradise is a garden in a corner of Eden, surrounded by fruit trees. As Satan approaches, he smells the delicious scent of the trees. One epic simile compares the perfume to the spicy odors which sailors smell off the coast of Arabia; a second contrasts it with the smell of burning fish which drove away the devil Asmodeus in a Hebrew fable.

Satan isn't deterred by the tangle of bushes and undergrowth that guards Paradise. He simply leaps over into the garden, his entrance celebrated in two more epic similes: Satan is like a wolf preying on sheep and like a burglar breaking in through a window. Once inside the garden, he perches on the Tree of Life in the shape of a cormorant.

He has chosen a good spot to survey Paradise, which lies open before him. It is watered by a river which runs south through Eden and comes up in Paradise as a fountain, then pours out again into four rivers. Next to Satan's perch is the Tree of Knowledge. In front of him are all the delights of Paradise: flowers, fruit, grazing animals, waterfalls, singing birds. Everything is so perfect that roses don't even have thorns. No garden famous in classical myth can compare with this "Assyrian garden" (Eden and Paradise were located in Mesopotamia). Satan glowers on this perfection, for he "Saw undelighted all delight."

Lines 288–410. Satan Sees Adam and Eve

We first see Adam and Eve through Satan's eyes. They walk naked and majestic through the Garden, exemplifying the order and harmony of God's creation. They are not equal, for Eve is subordinate to Adam and wears her hair longer, curling like tendrils of a vine that needs a tree for support.

The relationship between Adam and Eve is one of the most difficult ideas in *Paradise Lost* for us to accept. Adam is Eve's God: "He for God only, she for God in him: / His fair large front and eye sublime declared / Absolute rule." Christian marriage for Milton was not a partnership of equals but a harmonious hierarchy in which man and woman have different roles. Keep this in mind as the story unfolds, for Eve's sin is that she takes over leadership from Adam and Adam's sin is that he lets her do it.

Adam and Eve sit down to a vegetarian supper, watching the animals who play for their delight. Even the elephant gambols, though a bit ponderously.

Satan, watching from the Tree of Life, is consumed with envy. He comforts himself with the thought of dragging mankind away from Paradise to Hell. "There will be room / Not like these narrow limits, to receive / Your numerous offspring."

But don't blame me, Satan says. Blame God who made me seek revenge. Here you'll probably think of those people you know who always find someone or something else responsible for their actions, never themselves.

Satan now assumes the shape of different animals, getting closer and closer to Adam and Eve until he can hear their conversation.

Lines 411–775. Evening in Paradise

In Adam's first speech, he mentions God's prohibition against eating the fruit of the Tree of Knowledge. He doesn't know what Death is because (as you remember from Book II) Death is coming behind Satan and has not yet reached earth. Eve recounts the story of her birth from Adam's rib, acknowledging "How beauty is excelled by manly grace / And wisdom, which alone is truly fair." They embrace, making Satan furious with envy. He can only feel desire, never satisfaction—and his unsatisfied desire is the Hell he carries with him.

Satan has gained an important piece of information from his eavesdropping: he can corrupt man through the Tree of Knowledge. He voices the question that has probably already occurred to you: is man's happiness dependent on ignorance? As twentieth-century readers, we're likely to be scornful of a theology which seems to reward ignorance. But perhaps some kinds of knowledge are best left unknown: would man be happier if physicists had not used their knowledge to construct a nuclear bomb?

A plan to inflame Adam and Eve's desire for knowledge begins to form in Satan's mind as he moves off to look for an angel who might tell him more.

The setting sun suddenly illumines the eastern gate of Paradise (the only legitimate entrance), where the angel Gabriel is on guard between pillars of alabaster and rock. Uriel slides down a sunbeam and quickly warns Gabriel that one of the "banished crew" has deceived him and entered Paradise. Gabriel replies that nothing has entered through the gate, but he can't be sure that a spirit hasn't leapt over the surrounding hedge. However, if Satan is in the garden, Gabriel will know by morning.

Evening comes on, the nightingale begins to sing, and Adam suggests to Eve that they go early to bed in order to rest for their gardening chores. Eve reiterates her submission—"God is thy law, thou mine"—and asks Adam to explain why the stars and moon shine throughout the night when nothing can see them.

They prevent the world from reverting to the reign of Night, Adam explains, and they give light to millions of nocturnal spirits, who praise God continually. Talking together, Adam and Eve walk hand in hand to a flowery shelter, their marriage bed. In an epic simile, Eve is described as more lovely than Pandora, who in classical myth opened a box which brought sin and trouble to mankind. By now you're probably wondering what Milton has against women: for him, their beauty is certainly not an unmixed blessing.

Adam and Eve make their evening prayer to God who has blessed them with perfection. They go to bed in each other's arms, as Milton praises "wedded love." To enjoy its sensual pleasures is to obey God's law. True love is found in the sexual embraces of married lovers, not "in the bought smile / Of harlots, loveless, joyless, unendeared."

Lines 776–1015. Gabriel Confronts Satan

The angelic guards are posted to watch for the intruder. Ithuriel and Zephon are given the job of searching the bower where Adam and Eve are asleep.

They find Satan almost at once, squatting in the shape of a toad by Eve's ear. As soon as Ithuriel touches him with his spear, Satan springs up in his own shape. The transformation looks like an explosion, as the epic simile tells you.

Now we have come to one of the most dramatic passages in *Paradise Lost*. To get its full flavor, read it like a play, assigning roles to different speakers. Milton's skill in writing lines of blank verse is at its best here.

At first the two angels don't recognize Satan, causing him to reply scornfully, "Know ye not me?" You must be really low in the heavenly pecking order not to recognize me.

Zephon answers scorn with scorn: you don't look like a glorious angel now, you look like a creature from Hell. The rebuke stings Satan: he "felt how awful goodness is" (using "awful" in the sense of awe-inspiring).

When they bring Satan to where Gabriel has just met the other guards, Gabriel asks him why he has left Hell to make mischief in Paradise. Satan thinks it's a silly question—who wouldn't try to leave Hell? Yes, he was there beside Eve who was asleep, but that doesn't mean anything.

Gabriel answers sarcastically that Heaven lost a good judge of wisdom when it lost Satan, and that his smartness will get him sent back to Hell to learn better. Why is Satan alone? Gabriel asks.

Satan gets angry and calls his former comrade "Insulting Angel," and he boasts of his leadership in taking on the dangerous spying mission. He scoffs at the "gay legions" in Heaven who take the easy way and cringe before God instead of fighting against his tyranny.

Gabriel objects to Satan's using the word "faithful" of himself and his actions. Gabriel even accuses him of having flattered God with his fawning and cringing, hoping to take over God's throne. When finally he gets down to business, he threatens Satan that he will drag him in chains back to Hell and seal it over, if he finds him in Paradise again. Satan has the last word, defying Gabriel to capture him without another War in Heaven.

At this the angels surrounding Satan turn bright red and tighten their circle around him. There are so many of them and they stand so upright that their spears look like a field of wheat waiting to be cut. For his part, Satan draws himself up so that he looks like a mountain whose top reaches the sky. His helmet is proudly crested, and he seems to carry powerful weapons. It is a tense moment: will another war break out to tear apart not only Paradise but Heaven itself?

God doesn't want it to happen. He sends a miraculous sign from Heaven, holding in the sky the astrological sign Libra, the Balance, which God had used during the creation to equalize earth and air. In one side of the balance God places the consequences of leaving the place quietly; in the other, the consequences of fighting. Fighting proves lighter, which means less sensible: "The latter quick flew up and kicked the beam."

Look, Gabriel says, God doesn't want another fight. Neither of them can do what God denies, although the sign clearly shows that Satan is a lightweight compared to Gabriel. Satan leaves hastily, as the night gives way to dawn.

BOOK V

Lines 1–219. Morning in Paradise

Adam awakes, surprised to find that Eve is still asleep. After he wakes her gently, she tells him the dream which we know was put into her mind by the toad—Satan—who squatted by her head during the night.

Eve's dream foretells exactly what will happen. In it she hears a voice she thinks is Adam's, calling her to enjoy the night by walking to the Tree of Knowledge. There she meets an angel who plucks fruit from the Tree, using the argument that knowledge should not be forbidden to man. He offers Eve the fruit, promising that it will make her into a goddess. The fruit is so marvelously appetizing that she tastes it, and immediately she is given knowledge of the earth by seeing it from the clouds, as a goddess would. The dream ends as the guide disappears and Eve finds herself back in Paradise, asleep.

Although Adam comforts her, he is puzzled by the work of evil in a being who is "Created pure." Then he explains how dreams happen. His explanation is the first of what you may think of as the lectures of Book V. These lectures are Milton's version of the psychology and cosmology underlying *Paradise Lost*. You will be surprised at the variety of thinking in these lectures. The explanation of dreams, for example, is not far from current theory. But the hierarchy by which all lower things, even the planets, feed the higher ones, will strike you as medieval.

The explanation of dreams is not unlike one you may have heard, once you change a few terms. For Milton, Reason is the chief mental faculty, assisted by Fancy (imagination), which works on the input given by the senses. When we sleep, Fancy escapes from the control of Reason and produces "Wild work," with actions and ideas jumbled and mismatched. You may recognize similarities in this explanation to the Freudian scheme in which the unconscious expresses desires in dreams, when it escapes from the restraining influence of the waking consciousness.

Milton says that the past becomes present in dreams, a fact which makes Adam think that Eve's dream was caused by their evening discussion of the Tree of Knowledge. Of course we know better: we know as Adam doesn't that Satan put the dream in Eve's head. Adam hopes (but not with complete confidence) that she would never do what she had dreamed. This irony is a little heavy-handed, you may think.

Adam kisses away Eve's tears, and they go out to make their morning prayer, which consists of requests that all parts of the universe will join with them in praising God. Then they begin their gardening chores.

Lines 219–307. God Sends Raphael to Visit Adam and Eve

God sends Raphael down to warn Adam and Eve about the threat posed by Satan. Raphael is to make it clear to Adam that his fate is in his own hands because his will is free. But it is only fair to warn him, so that he cannot claim he is "unadmonished, unforewarned."

As Raphael flies to the gate of heaven and looks down on the earth below, Milton seizes the opportunity to mention Galileo again. But Galileo's knowledge of what he sees through his telescope is "less assured" than Raphael's, for Galileo is only human.

Raphael seems like a Phoenix as he flies down and lands on the eastern edge of the garden. The description will remind you of the figure of Mercury, which you can see on advertisements for flower delivery services, when Raphael folds his three pairs of wings, one pair attached to his heels. He walks majestically through the ranks of the angels guarding Paradise, then through a grove of spice trees perfuming the air. Adam sees Raphael coming as he sits waiting for Eve to prepare another vegetarian meal.

Lines 308–450. Adam and Eve Entertain Raphael

Adam calls to Eve to prepare a special meal with the best food and drink. Raphael approaches alone with great dignity, and here Milton makes a comment aside to the reader: he contrasts Raphael's composure with the "tedious pomp that waits / On Princes." A few years before *Paradise Lost* was written, King Charles II had entered London with great processions and parades. Since Milton had opposed the restoration of the monarchy, he was inclined to speak sourly of royal display.

Raphael, Adam, and Eve gather round a "grassy turf" to eat what seems to be a sumptuous picnic. Milton adds a domestic note: when you eat fruit and drink juice, there is "No fear lest dinner cool."

Raphael delivers another of Book V's lectures, this time on the universal need for nourishment. There is a vertical order which causes all lower things to become food for higher ones. Even the elements of earth, air, fire, and water feed the moon, which then sends out nourishment to the higher planets. In return for giving light to everything, the sun sucks up the humidity which rises. Saying that the food on earth compares well to that available in heaven, Raphael eats enthusiastically and digests his food as other creatures do, thus demonstrating that angels have a bodily existence.

Lines 451–561. After-Dinner Conversation in Paradise

Seeing that Raphael has enjoyed his dinner, Adam leads the conversation into a comparison of life in Heaven and on earth. Raphael, the celestial schoolteacher, provides information on the natural order. Everything begins the same, then becomes more refined as it approaches God. Even the flowers are more spiritual than the roots of a plant. When man eats the fruits, the nourishment produces the "vital spirits," life, sense, fancy, and understanding, which make the soul reasonable. Reason is the ruling faculty for both men and angels, but angels have "intuitive" reason (*line 488*), which means they understand at once, while man has "discursive" reason: he has to work things out logically. The food Raphael eats on earth is of the same kind as that in Heaven, but less refined because of its greater distance from God.

However—and there's irony in this—if Adam and Eve "be found obedient," they will probably become angels too and understand more than their human reason presently allows them.

Adam notices the fatal phrase and asks innocently how they can disobey a God who has been so good to them. Raphael offers another lecture, this one on the free will given to man by God. You'll recognize the main ideas from God's explanation of free will in Book III. God has given man and angels free will so that they can demonstrate their obedience: "freely we serve / Because we freely love." But already some have disobeyed and fallen into Hell.

Naturally Adam wants to know the whole story, since until this time he hadn't understood his situation or any of the history of the War in Heaven and his subsequent creation.

Lines 561–656. Raphael's Story

You have now come to the point in the narrative
where the story turns back to the events which came
before those of the first book. Raphael is about to tell
Adam and Eve how the War in Heaven happened
and what were its consequences. The story will take
up the rest of Book V and the whole of Books VI, VII,
and VIII. (We return to the present in Book IX.)

This story-within-a-story technique is easy enough
for us to follow because we're familiar with it from
movies and TV drama. But you should note that it's
another device Milton uses to put himself in the great
epic tradition. In Virgil's *Aeneid*, Aeneas the hero
relates the fall of Troy; in *The Odyssey*, Odysseus tells
King Alcinous his adventures during the ten years
since he left Troy.

Raphael takes his listeners, Adam and Eve, back to
a time when "this world was not, and Chaos wild /
Reigned where these Heavens now roll." (Remember
that in Book II King Chaos complained he had lost
part of his territory when God scooped up a piece of
Chaos to make the World.) At this time the Heavens
are about to celebrate the Great Year, which, according to the Greek philosopher Plato, comes every
36,000 years. (It takes that number of years for all the
heavenly spheres to complete all their revolutions.)
God is going to mark this Great Year with a special
proclamation: his Son is equal with himself. He calls
his Son "anointed," which is the meaning of the
Hebrew word "Messiah."

The announcement causes great rejoicing in Heav-
en, with music, dancing, and feasting "with Angels'
food." Finally all the hosts of angels retire to sleep in
their tents, while some remain awake singing hymns
of praise all night long.

Lines 657–802. Satan Assembles His Forces

Satan is also awake, but he isn't singing praises. He is stung with envy and hatred because another angel—not him—has been declared coequal with God. He is plotting how to strike back.

It isn't hard to identify with Satan's feelings. In fact, it's really more difficult to understand why God so abruptly elevated the Son, without explanation to Lucifer, as Satan was known in Heaven. We are given no reasons for God's preference. But that is part of what Milton wants us to understand about his God: we all must accept with obedience and grace whatever he decides.

Lucifer can't accept it. He feels like a child rejected in favor of another sibling. You may perhaps be familiar with another evil figure, Iago in Shakespeare's *Othello*. Iago's only motivation for the terrible destruction he brings about is that Othello promoted someone else instead of him. In Iago's case, like Lucifer's, the fury seems out of all proportion to the apparent cause.

Lucifer was "of the first / If not *the* first Archangel." Now he will be the first in opposition to God's will. He whispers to his closest companions a command to bring their forces to the North, the region traditionally connected with Satan. They will gather there to prepare a special welcome for the Son, he says.

But God is not deceived. As one-third of the angels follow Lucifer (now Satan), God warns his Son that a great battle is coming. The Son—in sharp contrast to Satan—never argues or contradicts his Father but assures him he will be equal to the challenge.

So, Raphael continues (using Adam's name in line 751 to remind us that we're following a story within a story), Satan took his numberless army to the North, where he set up a palace in imitation of the Mount of God. Satan addresses his followers, using the great line naming all the orders of angels: "Thrones, Dominations, Princedoms, Virtues, Powers." These impressive titles may not mean much now that the Son has usurped "All Power." How can we get free of their power, which was bad enough with one supreme authority and is unendurable now that God is double? His argument is based on the meaning of "peer," which means an equal. (Peers in a kingdom are those people equal to the king in political importance.) Satan's equality with God has been violated.

Lines 803–907. The Loyal Angel

One angel interrupts indignantly. Abdiel cannot bear to hear God blasphemed as a tyrant. Who is Satan to dispute God about liberty? Because God has elevated one of the angels to become his coequal, he has honored all of them. Better to seek forgiveness while there is some chance of getting it.

Satan scorns the suggestion that the Son had anything to do with Satan's origins—as he must have if he is God. (You will remember from the note on the Christian Trinity that all three parts of God exist from the beginning, and therefore the Son, as part of God, must have created the angels, Lucifer among them.) "We know no time when we were not as now." Angels are "self-begot, self-raised," and therefore they owe their origin to no one else. Abdiel is told to take this defiance back to God before anything worse happens.

Abdiel seems like the good guy who stands up to the gang leaders. He knows what's right and will not put up with anything illegal. You can admire his courage when you think of someone being surrounded by an armed crowd of ruthless bullies.

Milton probably thought of himself as Abdiel, the lonely defender of the truth. Even during the republic, when the Puritans held power, he was an individualist whose views were regarded as extreme. When he wrote *Paradise Lost,* he felt utterly isolated among the Royalists who came in with King Charles II and restored not only the monarchy but religious ceremonies that Milton despised. "Among the faithless, faithful only he": this comes from Milton's heart.

BOOK VI

This is the Star Wars book of *Paradise Lost.* It's the War in Heaven, with two armies of angels battling each other on the ground and above it. Telling this story presents the same technical challenges as recounting an outer-space battle in modern science fiction.

The background is entirely imaginary and not entirely clear. (See if you can draw a picture of Heaven from the description given in this book.) An imaginary setting gives the writer unlimited possibilities, but it doesn't make it easy for you to visualize. You can't feel familiar with a landscape that you can't connect with a place you have seen.

Keep in mind another fact: none of the angels in the battle can die. That may be nice for them, but it cuts down drastically on the range of emotions the story can evoke. We can't feel the pathos of a young warrior's death or the suspense of a last-minute rescue.

In the circumstances, the War in Heaven is about as exciting as it can be. Look for the invention of gunpowder on the second day and the terrifying scene on

the third day when the rebels are pushed off the edge
of Heaven. Read the book quickly to get its swift
action.

Lines 1–201. Abdiel's Courage

Through the night, Abdiel runs back to the Mount
of God, expecting to bring news of Satan's rebellion.
But the news is already known, and preparations are
well in hand. God praises Abdiel from inside a golden
cloud, telling him that he has won the more difficult
battle—the moral one—by standing up for the right.
Now comes the easier fight.

Commanded by Michael and Gabriel, the army of
God marches out in perfect order. The angels fly
above the ground like the birds who came to get their
names from Adam. Remember that Raphael is telling
the story to Adam; this is why he uses "thee" in line
75.

The armies meet each other after marching a distance ten times longer than the earth. (This is certainly
an imaginary battlefield!) Satan descends from his
gold chariot and walks toward the army of God.
Abdiel cannot bear to see Satan's pride and speaks to
himself in a speech called a "soliloquy." In his soliloquy, Abdiel resolves to attack Satan, arguing that he
should be able to win a physical fight after winning
the moral one. So Abdiel becomes the champion of
God's army, the first to strike the rebel Lucifer.

Lines 202–405. The First Day of the War in Heaven

As the war rages on and above the ground, Lucifer
fights fiercely, defeating all who come near him.
When he sees the archangel Michael cutting down

squadrons of the rebel angels with the sword he swings in two hands, Satan thrusts his great shield (remember from Book I that it is as big as the moon) between the sword and its intended victims. Michael challenges him to single combat.

It is a battle like that between two planets. Each has almighty power, but Michael has the advantage of a tempered sword. He chops Satan's sword in half and then pierces Satan's side as he lifts his sword arm. "Then Satan first knew pain," as a stream of liquid pours from the wound.

Of course he soon recovers; he is an angel who "Cannot but by annihilating die." Moloch suffers an even more terrible wound soon after, when he is split down to the waist by Gabriel. But again it's not fatal.

It is becoming clear that the rebel angels are getting the worst of the battle. The heavenly forces retain their discipline: "In cubic phalanx firm advanced entire." Their strength comes from their discipline because they have not sinned and disobeyed.

Lines 406–669. The Second Day

The war stops for the night, but Satan does not rest. He calls a council to discuss their next move. We now know something about his debating style: he's going to be asked a question to which he conveniently has the answer. Nisroc obliges. He cannot stand pain, the new discovery, and wants to know if there is any weapon which would inflict some of it on their enemy.

It's already invented, Satan says. Beneath the surface (remember, this isn't the earth!) are the makings of gunpowder. We shall overwhelm God's forces with a new weapon, the cannon. Raphael, turning to Adam, who listens intently to the story, remarks that the angels recognized what a simple idea it was once they had been told about it. For us twentieth-century readers, Raphael's remark that man may just as easily invent more terrible instruments of war is heavily ironical.

The "victor angels" rise next morning and scout for their enemy. The cherub Zophiel brings the news that the rebels are advancing, closely packed. They are hiding the cannon, but the heavenly host doesn't know that yet.

Satan delivers a speech full of puns. On the surface it seems he is talking about offers of peace, but every word has two meanings: "composure" means the composition of gunpowder as well as a truce; "overture" is not the beginning of negotiations, as the heavenly host is intended to think, but the opening blast from the cannon; "discharge," "in charge," "touch," "propound," and "loud" all have two meanings.

Raphael tells what he saw, because of course he was there: as the ranks of the rebel angels divided in two, the heavenly host saw what looked like pillars laid in rows on wheels. Behind each "pillar" stood an angel with a lighted torch, who touched off the gunpowder.

The effect is all that the rebel angels hoped for. As the enemy are blasted off their feet, "By thousands, angel on archangel rolled." The heavenly host are routed and rendered helpless, to the amusement of Satan and his friends. He and Belial enjoy themselves in two more speeches full of fairly tedious puns.

The heavenly host finally pulls itself together and makes a somewhat surprising counterattack. They pull up hills and throw them on top of the rebel angels. The weight of the mountains causes their armor to cut into their flesh painfully. Although they are spirits and logically shouldn't be capable of being imprisoned under heavy weights, their sins have made their spirits heavy, and it's not so easy for them to get out.

Meanwhile, those rebel angels who haven't been caught by flying mountains adopt the trick themselves. "So hills amid the air encountered hills," as Heaven is torn up in a horrifying chaos which seems worse than war itself.

Lines 670–747. God Intervenes

God has been watching the dreadful destruction. He permits it in order to enhance the glory of his Son, who will bring the conflict to an end. He tells the Son about the events of the first two days and says that he has reserved the third for him: "that the Glory may be thine / Of ending this great war, since none but Thou / Can end it." He commands him to lead out all the heavenly forces and drive the rebel angels down to Hell.

The Son accepts the command willingly, again making a clear contrast between his obedience and Satan's rebellion. For the Son, "to obey is happiness entire."

Do you feel that the Son is just too good to be true? It's difficult to feel in awe of him because he tends to sound like a kid who wants to please authority. But you might ask yourself how a writer can portray goodness in the abstract. What could Milton do to make the Son as interesting as Satan is?

Lines 748–892. The Third Day

God's chariot rushes out as soon as the third day dawns. It is magnificently decorated with jewels; flames surround a sapphire throne on which the Son rides, with the allegorical figure of Victory at his right hand. He is accompanied by "ten thousand thousand saints," a contrast to the weary soldiers under Michael's command. The two forces combine to make an army of unimaginable size. As the Son and the Army advance, the hills uprooted in the previous day's fighting return miraculously to their places and the flowers grow again.

Satan's forces also regroup, "hope conceiving from despair." They make themselves ready for a battle they know must be final. The Son tells his forces to stand aside—this battle is his. The war was caused by Lucifer's injured pride when God elevated his Son, so it is right that the Son alone should fight the last fight: "against me is all their rage."

The sweeping of the fallen angels out of Heaven is the most thrilling action of the War in Heaven. The invention of gunpowder has its comic apsects, but the sweep stretches the imagination. Read it out loud to get the excitement of the images and the sound effects.

The four cherubs on the Son's chariot spread their wings, and the chariot charges on the enemy. The rebel angels drop their weapons in horror as the chariot rides over them: "O'er shields and helms and helmed heads he rode / Of Thrones and mighty Seraphim prostrate." He uses no more than half of his forces; he doesn't want to destroy the angels but to push them out of Heaven.

He drives them before him like a herd of frightened goats, to the "Crystal wall of Heaven," which opens on Chaos. The rebel angels look out with horror, but they are so terrified of the Son in his flaming chariot that they throw themselves down.

They fall for nine days through Chaos, who objects loudly to their huge number. He knows that he will lose a lot of territory to house them in Hell.

Hell closes on the rebels, now the fallen angels, while in Heaven the faithful angels repair the gap in the crystal wall and the Son returns to the honor of a seat on God's right hand.

Lines 893–912. Raphael's Warning to Adam

Now, Raphael says to Adam, you know how Satan got into Hell. But he is "now plotting how he may seduce / Thee also from obedience." Satan intends to make man share his eternal misery in Hell in order to revenge himself on God. Be careful, Adam, Raphael warns: do not listen to his temptations. And warn Eve. She is "Thy weaker." Remember the example of the fallen angels, who suffered because of their disobedience.

BOOK VII

Lines 1–39. The Invocation for the Second Half of *Paradise Lost*

Book VII marks the beginning of the second half of the poem, so another invocation to Urania is in order. "Half yet remains unsung," Milton says, but this half won't take him to such giddy heights in the cosmos because the action will take place mostly on earth.

As you saw in the previous invocations, they give Milton a chance to talk about himself. Here he portrays himself as alone, blind ("In darkness"), "fallen

on evil days," and "with dangers compassed round."
For Milton, the restoration of the monarchy under
King Charles II meant forced retirement from public
life and the danger of personal reprisal from the vic-
torious Royalists. A number of his friends suffered
cruel deaths. He thought of the king's party as "Bac-
chus and his revellers," who tore apart the poet
Orpheus in a drunken orgy. He hopes to find a few
readers who can appreciate what he has to say: "fit
audience find, though few."

The Rest of Book VII

We are now back at the point where Book I began.
But the flashback isn't complete yet. While the rebel
angels were falling through Chaos and lying chained
on the burning lake in Hell, God created the World.

The whole of Book VII is a retelling in frequently
delightful poetry of the Hebrew creation myth found
in the Book of Genesis, Chapter 1 and the first three
verses of Chapter 2. Read them parallel with Book VII
so that you can see where Milton uses the same words
and where he embroiders an idea suggested in Genesis.

There is one important difference you may have
noticed from this telling of the myth and Milton's. In
Paradise Lost it is God the Son who goes down to the
World and creates all things. As you know from the
note on Christian theology in Book III, the Holy Trinity existed from the first, in a mystic whole-and-part
relationship. When the Hebrew creation myth was
written, God was single, as he still is in the Judaic
religion.

But Milton isn't really clear about which aspect of
God actually performs the creation. God takes the gol-

den compasses *(line 225)* to carve the world out of Chaos, and it isn't obvious that the Son is meant here. In fact, when the Son returns to Heaven in triumph, Milton admits that God the Father had been along all the time: "for he also went / Invisible, yet stayed (such privilege / Hath Omnipresence)".

You might want to consider the difficulties Milton has in making details like this logically consistent. Think of it this way: we now have a physical explanation for the universe; we can deduce the origins of matter and life from scientific observations. We don't attribute moral qualities to the universe. Our explanation is objective and neutral.

But Milton saw the universe and its creation as moral acts. From the physical universe he deduced a necessary pattern of man's moral behavior. The Christian Son of God, with his sacrifice for mankind's sake, had to be part of the essential structure of the universe. Nothing is morally neutral, for everything speaks to us of God's goodness and reminds us of our place in the universe and the responsibilities due to that place.

It's worth pointing out that Milton was trying to do something we don't attempt any more. We now attribute moral behavior entirely to our need to live together peaceably for everyone's benefit.

Book VII is a joyous interlude after the noise and terror of the War in Heaven and before the anguish of Adam and Eve's temptation. Just enjoy it. Read it fast for the sweep of the creation and the pleasure of the details—the "fish that with their fins and shining scales / Glide under the green wave"; the whale who "at his trunk spouts out a sea"; and the mole throwing little hills of dirt behind him as he digs.

BOOK VIII

This book is the final part of the flashbacks. Adam tells Raphael of his own experiences when Eve was given to him. Life in Paradise is at its most idyllic here, just before the great catastrophe in Book IX. Because of what is soon to happen, Adam's happiness, so movingly expressed, has a pathetic irony.

Lines 1–178. Astrophysical Theories

Adam detains Raphael with a question about the motion of the planets. Wouldn't it seem more economical to have the earth move instead of the sun, which works very hard to give the earth its light?

As Raphael prepares to answer, Eve slips away to work in her flower garden. She prefers to hear these explanations from Adam, who "would intermix / Grateful digressions" and use his lips for other actions besides talking. In this book Eve behaves exactly as she should—in sharp contrast to the next book.

Raphael's explanation shows that Milton was completely aware of ancient and modern cosmological theories. God, the "great Architect," has not made his secrets easy for men to ferret out. In fact, he's probably laughing at the details of the Ptolemaic scheme: "With centric and eccentric scribbled over / Cycle and epicycle, orb in orb."

The universe was built by God for his own purposes, and man is "lodged in a small partition." Raphael expounds Copernican cosmology in a passage which is now very difficult to follow because it contains terminology we no longer use. The point is that it doesn't matter if the sun "Rise on the earth or earth rise on the sun." In any case, these matters are God's business and not man's: "be lowly wise: / Think only what concerns thee and thy being."

NOTE: Humanism   You might be surprised that
Milton seems to be putting restrictions on inquiry. But
that's not really what he's saying. He admired Galileo,
as you have seen, which shows his interest in science.
Milton is advocating the kind of studies we now call
"humanities" and which were called "humanism" in
the Renaissance. Humanism is contrasted with the
obscure metaphysical discussions which occupied
medieval theologians. Milton is putting into Raphael's
mouth the argument for man and man's concerns as
the highest good. It was this humanism which led to
the great scientific discoveries of the eighteenth century, because humanism fixed men's minds on this
world, not on those "other worlds, what creatures
there / Live, in what state, condition, or degree."

Lines 179–451. Adam and God

Adam wants to talk further with Raphael, so he
flatters him by saying that he can never get enough of
his words' "sweetness." There is a nice little angelic
joke when Raphael says that he'd be glad to hear
about Adam's first experiences, because at the time of
Adam's creation, Raphael was on guard duty outside
Hell, seeing that no devils disturbed the creation.
Raphael even heard the noise in Pandemonium as the
fallen angels debated.

But Adam's speech is not in the poem for the information it gives. The material all comes from Chapter 2
of the Book of Genesis, so there's nothing new in it—
certainly not for an omniscient angel! What it estab-
lishes is the relationship between Adam, representing
man, and God.

God created man like himself—"in his own
image"—so naturally he gave him no mate. This left
Adam with no one to talk to. The beasts are lower in

the hierarchy and therefore no fit company for man. God complains that he himself is "alone / From all eternity, for none I know / Second to me or like, equal much less." Yes, Adam says, but you, God, can raise any member of your creation up to your own status whenever you want company; I can't.

Finally God agrees to give Adam his heart's desire, but only because Adam has passed the test of self-knowledge.

This conversation has given us two pieces of information: man is higher than the beasts but lower than God, and God sets up tests to see whether man will pass them. Adam passes this one, but he will fail in the next book.

Lines 451–653. Marriage and Paradise

Do you know the word "uxorious"? It comes from the Latin "uxor," the word for "wife," and it is used to describe a man who is under his wife's domination (not henpecked—that's too small an idea). Adam comes dangerously close to uxoriousness in his adoration of Eve.

He has some excuse for his extreme love, for she was formed from a part of his own body. No other couple can possibly enjoy such closeness. Adam knows very well that she is intended to be his inferior, that she is less like God than he is. But this means nothing when Eve is near. What she wants to do or say "seems wisest, virtuousest, discreetest, best." She knows more than knowledge, is wiser than wisdom, has greatness of mind and "nobleness" as well.

Raphael isn't entirely pleased to hear Adam's extravagant praise of his wife. Adam, he says, don't be unwise in overvaluing what your better judgment tells you is "less excellent." Eve is to be loved, but she must not rule. Sexual love should also not be overvalued, for animals reproduce in the same way and are lower in the universal order. Adam must love with reason, as suits a man.

Adam feels the force of this rebuke and hastens to assure Raphael that it is not Eve's body but her character which enchants him: "those graceful acts / Those thousand decencies that daily flow / From all her words and actions." He turns to Raphael: since love is the highest emotion and leads to Heaven, do angels love? And if they do, can they touch?

Raphael blushes as he explains that angels need no physical apparatus to express their love. With relief, he points out to Adam that the sun is going down and he must leave. He delivers a final summary of the advice he has given Adam throughout their long conversation (it has lasted more than three books of the poem) and departs.

BOOK IX

Lines 1–47. The Introduction

This book, where the central action occurs, begins with a statement that we are now coming to the tragic climax: "I now must change / These notes to tragic." He thinks his "sad task" more heroic, meaning more worthy of epic treatment, than *The Iliad* or *The Odyssey* because of the importance of his story. He hopes he can rise to the occasion with the help of Urania, who visits him each night with her inspiration.

Milton says that he looked for a long time for the right subject for his epic poem. He didn't want to write about wars but about something of worldwide significance. His subject—the Fall of man—is enough by itself to be called heroic; he hopes he will be able to do justice to it, unless he is too old or too sick. He certainly can't do it without the help of Urania each night. (You will remember from the invocation to Book III that Milton composed *Paradise Lost* each night and then dictated it in the morning.)

Lines 47–191. Satan Enters the Serpent

Satan has been circling the earth for seven days and nights. Finally, on the eighth night, he slips through the guardian angels. Paradise, as we said before, was in Mesopotamia, the land between the rivers Tigris and Euphrates. Satan went in with Tigris where it flowed underground and came up with the river when it became a fountain in Paradise, near the Tree of Life.

The places he has been are listed in a catalog of place names, ranging from Eden through the river Ob in Siberia and back to India, a list meant to impress with the range of Satan's wanderings. He has decided to use "The serpent, subtlest beast of all the field," for his evil purposes.

As he prepares to enter the snake's body, Satan expresses his "inward grief." This speech, addressed first to the earth and then becoming a soliloquy about his feelings, is essential to an understanding of Satan's character. Read it with the psychological insight you'd use if you were discussing someone you know. It is a dramatic presentation of the confused and contradictory feelings people have when they are so frustrated that they want to do something reckless.

Watch the shift in Satan's focus as his feelings change. First he admires the earth, at the center of the universe, receiving light from all the other heavenly bodies. How pleasant it would have been for Satan to live on earth, but instead "the hateful siege / Of contraries" increases his torments. The only way to resolve his contradictory feelings is to destroy man. Then he will be able to say that he has spoiled in one day what it took God six days to create.

The thought of God shifts his focus to his near victory: almost half of the angels followed him in Heaven rather than God. Satan attributes the creation of man to God's need to replace the numbers of angels lost.

He returns briefly to the magnificence of the World and the angels guarding it. His pride makes him sympathize with what he thinks is the indignity of service. Pride also causes him anguish at having to use the serpent, "bestial slime," as a hiding place to elude the angels.

But he will do anything for revenge, despite his understanding that revenge "back on itself recoils." His final focus is on spite, the meanest kind of revenge.

He finds the serpent and enters through his mouth. Until this moment, the serpent was as innocent as any other creature: "Fearless unfeared he slept." With details like this, Milton increases the sense of terrible impending tragedy which will spoil the innocence of everything forever.

Lines 191–384. The Fatal Decision

For the serpent to tempt Eve, he must have her on her own. In the Biblical source of the story there is no mechanism for Eve to become separated from Adam. In Milton's version, this dialog not only separates Adam and Eve, it also tells us about their relationship. You can see that the angel Raphael had reason to warn Adam against uxoriousness.

The arguments Eve makes are reasonable ones. So are Adam's replies. The dialog illustrates the old saying that the way to Hell is paved with good intentions.

Eve first argues for the division of labor: if we separate, we will get twice as much done. When we work together, we talk too much.

Adam gently points out that God won't really mind if all the garden chores do not get done. God didn't make man for toil, but for "delight / He made us, and delight to reason joined." If you really want to leave me for a little while, I won't mind—except for one thing: we have been warned of danger and should stay together.

This is not news to Eve, who had overheard the conversation between Adam and Raphael. But she is not pleased by the implication that she can't be trusted to repel the seducer.

Adam hastily assures her that he didn't mean she can't be trusted, but that Satan will be unlikely to attack if they are together. Even if you fight off the temptation, it is a horrible experience which you don't want to suffer if you can help it. He is a strong enemy, for he seduced half the angels. Stay with me, Eve: I am strengthened by your presence. Don't you feel the same?

But, Eve argues, Paradise isn't much if we have to stick together for fear of harm. God could not have "left so imperfect" the situation in Eden.

Adam severely puts Eve right, using the word "woman" instead of the usual flattering titles. God is perfect, but he left man free will. The responsibility is ours, so I am not mistrusting you, Eve, but simply taking sensible precautions. First prove your obedience. After all, if you repel the tempter alone, who will be there to see? Adam finally gives the responsibility to Eve: she has her own free will and must make her own choices. If she stays to please Adam, she would build up resentment. With a warning, he gives permission for her to go.

Eve has the last word, as Milton points out. She feels perfectly confident in her own powers, and she's convinced that Satan wouldn't attack the weaker of the two first. If he did, "the more shame his repulse."

Lines 385–493. Satan Watching Eve

They part, promising to meet for lunch. Milton addresses Eve directly as she walks away, innocent for the last time.

The serpent has found Eve alone. He watches her and smells her delicious perfume as she tends the plants. Her effect on Satan is expressed in a long and very famous epic simile, beginning with the line "As one who long in populous city pent." A city dweller breathes with pleasure the scents of the country air and finds a country girl so lovely that she "sums all delight." In fact, for a few moments, Eve's innocent beauty makes Satan "stupidly good."

But not for long. He hisses to himself that he has forgotten the main purpose of his journey, which is not to enjoy himself but to destroy others. Eve is alone, without the protection of her husband "Whose higher intellectual more I shun." His hate is stronger than her beauty.

Think back to Eve's boast and Satan's relief that he has found the weaker of the pair alone. The irony is almost unbearable.

Lines 494–790. The Tempting of Eve

This is the climax of *Paradise Lost*. In this dialog you see the tempter at his most subtle and Eve—representing woman—at her worst. It is a marvelously dramatic scene, with the tension increasing in every line. You begin to bite your nails with anxiety for Eve, wanting to shout at her that the serpent is getting at all her weakest points. By the end of the scene, it's all over. Everything in the world is downhill after this.

First the serpent gets Eve's attention by playing in front of her like all the other animals. Then he flatters her: every living thing adores your beauty, but they are all beasts and there is only one man to appreciate you. You should be a goddess because you are so beautiful.

Eve is a bit surprised that a serpent can talk, since speech was denied to animals at the creation. However, they often look and act like reasonable creatures. She asks the serpent to explain why he has suddenly become so friendly to her.

Watch how the serpent works on Eve's vanity. The serpent was the only animal who could reach the fruit of the tree, so there is something special about him. And then, after eating the fruit had made him wise and able to speak, his new wisdom made him appreciate Eve, "sovereign of creatures, universal dame." Is such flattery resistible? And is it a fair assumption that a woman always falls for it? Eve has no model of female behavior from which to learn or to compare herself with.

The serpent offers to show her the wonderful tree, and they set off together. An epic simile performs its usual function of intensifying the message: as the serpent leads Eve through the undergrowth, the jeweled crest on his head shines like those phosphorescent vapors which rise above bogs and marshes. People mistake them for lights and get drowned—exactly as Eve is going to be misled.

Eve is puzzled when she arrives with the serpent at the Tree of Knowledge. We can't touch this tree, she says. God commanded it. But notice carefully what she says next: except for this prohibition, we live according to the dictates of our reason, which is our law. The word "reason" is central to the serpent's argument with Eve's fatal decision. Reason is a fallible guide for mankind, who should trust God.

After Eve has reiterated God's prohibition (using the exact words of Genesis in lines 662 and 663), Satan seems to pull himself up and marshall all his forces like a classical orator preparing for a supreme speech. Satan's speech is a classic of persuasion.

The tree is the "mother of science," and he feels the power of knowledge within him. Eve—"Queen of the universe"—will not die. The fruit is life, knowledge—it cannot kill. Look at me: I ate it and here I am. Why does God deny to a man what a beast has tasted?

God must have prohibited the tree because he wanted no rivals. When a beast eats the fruit, he moves up the hierarchy and becomes human; so, logically, if a human eats the fruit, he will become a god. Using another logical argument, Satan asks what harm there is in man's having knowledge, since God has power over everything and will only give man knowledge of what he wills to. You need this fruit, Eve: "Goddess humane, reach then and freely taste."

And then Milton adds a stroke of genius that makes the story truly moving: Eve is already partly persuaded by those treacherous guides, logic and reason, but it's also lunchtime and she's hungry. You will sympathize with this—so often a tiny practical detail tips the balance when you're making a decision.

Eve's speech is full of logic and reason. If the tree protects the knowledge of good and evil, how can we know good without tasting the fruit? She raises the question which never receives a satisfactory answer: has God forbidden wisdom to man? The argument that convinces Eve is the sight of the serpent, obviously none the worse for having tasted the fruit. You will realize, as Eve does not, that the serpent is lying. He has never tasted the fruit. Do you think Eve even suspects that the serpent is really Satan in disguise?

Within two lines the deed is done: "she plucked, she ate." The earth shudders. The serpent slinks back to his cover while Eve gorges herself until she is drunk on the fruit.

Lines 795–999. Adam's Fall

The first thing Eve does after she has fallen to temptation is to worship the tree and the "sapience" (wisdom) it has given her. Instead of worshipping God in the morning, now she will care for the tree, praise it, and pick its fruit. Next she thanks experience for leading her to wisdom. In doing these things she is intensifying her sin because she is making the tree into her god instead of the true God. She now calls him the "great forbidder, safe with all his spies / About him."

Eve decides to share her gift with Adam, but her motive is impure, like all her thinking now. If she must die, having eaten of the Tree of Knowledge, and if Adam doesn't die but remains immortal, he will get another Eve. Much better to have Adam die too.

Adam has made her a garland of flowers for her hair, but he's worried. He goes to meet her and finds her coming from the Tree of Knowledge with a branch in her hand. We can only imagine his face as he sees that sight.

Eve spills out the whole story to him and urges him to eat so that they will be equal. If he doesn't, a difference in degree will divide them, for she does not want to renounce her newfound deity.

Adam drops the garland, transfixed with horror. He realizes who the serpent really is. In an internal soliloquy, he decides to join her because of his love. When he speaks aloud to Eve, he is surprisingly mild, for he recognizes that the deed cannot be undone. Perhaps God will not destroy us, he reasons, for to do so would give God a poor reputation in the eyes of Satan. In any case, Adam cannot be divided from Eve, for they are one flesh. Eve's answer includes the first time her action is named "guilt" and "crime." She too believes that Death will not come, for she feels full of life, "new hopes, new joys."

So he takes the fruit from her hand and eats. Again the earth trembles. Milton says that Adam ate the fruit

> Against his better knowledge, not deceived
> But fondly overcome with female charm.

His crime is different from Eve's: he did not succumb directly to the tempter but instead put Eve's love ahead of his duty to God. Both Adam and Eve have now pushed God away from his rightful place in their thoughts. In Eve's case, she worships a tree; in Adam's, he worships Eve.

Lines 1000–1189. Adam and Eve's First Quarrel

The only time that Milton uses the phrase "original sin" to describe the Fall is in the first lines after Adam has committed it. The sin is consummated with the first lustful copulation in Paradise. Adam and Eve behave like two people after a party, too drunk to care what they're doing.

When they've slept it off, they realize for the first time that they are naked. Despair settles on Adam as he reproaches Eve. How can he ever again talk with God and his angels in his shameful nakedness? He suggests that they find some way to cover themselves.

They use fig leaves from the Indian banyan tree. Now Adam and Eve look like the native Americans that Columbus found when he arrived in the New World.

Their sorry state causes them not only to weep but to feel anger, hate, mistrust, and suspicion for each other. They begin a miserable quarrel, full of the kind of reproaches which are perfectly true but of no help whatsoever in the present situation. If you hadn't eaten the fruit, Adam says to Eve, we'd still be happy. If you had commanded me not to leave you, Eve says, I wouldn't have done this. It's your fault.

Adam furiously replies that he won't take that responsibility—he couldn't force her against her free will. Perhaps I was a bit overconfident, but I'm sorry for it now, especially since you are accusing me of causing the whole mess. Any man who trusts a woman will not only get into trouble, he'll get blamed for it as well.

The quarrel goes on. It can't come to any conclusion because neither is willing to take responsibility. You will understand that from your own experience; noth-

ing improves until one party is willing to give a little
and then the other joins in. But it's deadlock until that
point.

BOOK X

The events in Book IX are like a spark causing the
explosion of reactions in Book X. We're going to see
the consequences of the Fall on earth, in Heaven, and
in Hell. The book contains an enormous variety of
action, from the building of the great bridge across
Chaos to the suicidal thoughts of Eve. You won't be
bored in this book, and you'll even find occasional
comic touches—for example, when Death complains
that there isn't much meat for him on earth with only
two people around.

Lines 1–228. The Son Judges Adam and Eve

The book opens with a moralizing summary of
what has happened. God allowed Satan to tempt Eve,
who in turn corrupted Adam. They had free will and
"ought to have still remembered" not to taste the fruit
no matter who suggested it. They are clearly guilty.
Now it remains to be seen how the penalty will be
inflicted.

The guardian angels have returned to Heaven
"mute and sad / For man," and a bit shamefaced
themselves, for they didn't catch Satan as he entered
Paradise. God, speaking from his cloud, absolves
them of blame, since nothing they could have done
would have prevented Satan from getting in.

At the same time he absolves himself from blame in
the Fall. He doesn't seem very sympathetic toward
Adam, who doesn't understand that Death will come,

even though it hasn't struck immediately. God sends the Son to judge Adam and Eve because that's appropriate to the Son's future role as man's redeemer.

The Son reminds himself that he himself will suffer the worst of these events, as he has promised to do. He will go alone to the Garden of Paradise, and the judgment will be a private matter.

The narrative of the judgment follows Genesis closely (in one case, word for word). Read it so that you can see the source of Adam and Eve's different answers. Adam doesn't come off very well: he blames Eve, and to some extent he blames God. *You* gave me this woman, he says, and you made her so perfect that I couldn't resist her.

Eve answers with simplicity, as she does in the Biblical account: "The serpent beguiled me and I did eat." With her admission of guilt and acceptance of responsibility, Eve regains some dignity.

The judgment on the serpent—that he and mankind will always be enemies—is followed by a flashforward to the time when the Son in his form as the man Jesus Christ will clean out Hell, fulfilling the punishment on the serpent.

Eve's punishment is the pain of childbirth and domination by her husband. Adam's is hard work. In Book IX, when Adam tried to persuade Eve not to be so compulsive about their work in the garden, he said that they were formed for delight, not work. The Fall has changed all that. Man is now made for work.

At least the instant stroke of Death has been "removed far off." The Son shows that other aspect of his role, service to man, as he provides clothes for Adam and Eve and inwardly gives them his own righteousness to conceal them from God's sight.

Lines 230–417. The Arrival of Sin and Death

We last saw Satan's daughter and son/grandson in Book II, when Satan left Hell. He hasn't returned since, though he has been in many other parts of the universe. Sin and Death think that no news is good news. Since he's been so long away, he must have been successful, and there will be prey for both of them.

Remember that Sin and Death are allegorical figures. When Sin says that she feels new strength within her, we understand that Sin is gaining from man's fall. She suggests building a path from Hell to the World, an allegorical way of implying that there'll be a lot of traffic both ways pretty soon.

Death is all for it. He can already smell his prey. They set off like two vultures who arrive on a battlefield the day before the fight—they know what's coming.

When they get out into Chaos, they collect all the solid material flying and floating around there and drive it back toward the mouth of Hell, like (another epic simile) winds from the North Pole driving icebergs to stop up the Northeast passage. Sin and Death make this material into a landing place anchored deep in the roots of Hell. Building from this "beach," they make a bridge right across Chaos, ending at the point on top of the world where Satan first looked down to the earth. (Recall Book III; this is the point where you can look up into Heaven, down into the World, and out into Chaos. The bridge is on the left of the universe in the diagram on page 28.)

Sin and Death are poised at that spot, their road

made behind them, when Satan arrives. He had hidden himself when the Son came down to judge him and Adam and Eve. He doesn't seem upset by the prophecy that mankind "will bruise his heel." He is too pleased with his success to worry much about what he thinks will be a punishment that lies far in the future.

Compare Satan's greeting of Sin here with their first meeting in Book II. Satan has become so deeply tainted by his destructive revenge that he greets the loathsome figure with joy. When he first saw her, he recoiled in shame from his connection with her.

Sin hails her father as victor: "Thine now is all the world." You're fully avenged for the defeat in Heaven, and God will have to divide his realm with you. It seems like a reasonable conclusion—one you might have reached yourself—yet this is only Book X; Books XI and XII will change things for Satan. But now he is triumphant as he delegates his reign on earth to Sin and Death. They go straight down through the spheres to earth, while Satan takes the high road across Chaos to Hell.

Lines 418–584. Serpents in Hell

At the beginning of this book the guardian angels returned to Heaven sad and ashamed that Satan had tricked them and entered Paradise. In contrast, when Satan arrives in Hell, he remains invisible while he takes his seat on his throne, and then he is suddenly revealed in what he thinks is glory but Milton despises as "false glitter." Satan is so sure that his victory has restored him to his former state that he calls the assembled fallen angels by that great rolling title, "Thrones, Dominations, Princedoms, Virtues, Powers."

His speech is a long boast about his accomplishments and how easy it was to seduce the new creation. He has done it all with an apple! God is so disproportionately angered that for one little apple he has given up his beloved man and his new World to Sin and Death. They're looking after the place until we can all get up there to rule over man. Satan doesn't think much of God's punishment:

> His seed, when is not set, shall bruise my head:
> A world who would not purchase with a bruise?

Satan himself can hardly be more surprised that we are at what happens next. All the devils in Pandemonium, including Satan, become serpents. Enjoy Milton's wonderful details as he describes an angel becoming a serpent, his face narrowing, his arms and legs becoming part of his body. Finally he falls on his belly. Read the whole passage aloud to hear the hissing that comes from all those "s" sounds. The catalog of classical serpents adds horror by association.

After the fallen angels become serpents, they climb a tree to get fruit and it turns to bitter ashes in their mouths. Milton tells us that the devils must assume the shape of snakes for a certain time each year to humble their pride. He refers to snake cults in classical Greek myth, suggesting that they arose through the connection of Satan and serpent.

NOTE: The Equation of Snakes with Devils   It is difficult for us to sympathize with the stigmatizing of one creature, the snake. We think of snakes as members of the reptile family with distinct and fascinating adaptations to survival in divergent habitats. But treating animals as being morally neutral is very modern. (It hasn't completely taken over yet; cockroaches are not regarded with detachment, even by sophisti-

cated people, when they share their kitchens!)
Snakes, serpents, worms, and dragons (a not quite
mythical variety of snakelike lizard) have had moral
and magical significance for almost all the world's religions. Milton's extreme antipathy stems more from
the snake's association with other religions than from
any feelings about the biological animal. Snakes represent the practices of religions that seduce weak people away from the true religion.

Lines 585–714. A Changed World

Here we are, Sin says to her son Death, what do
you think of this empire? Isn't this better than sitting
at the gate of Hell? Death replies that there don't seem
to be many pickings for him. Just wait a bit till I've
worked on man, Sin says, and you'll have plenty.
Meanwhile, work on everything else that lives—
plants, animals, fish, birds.

From this dialog we gather that Death came to
everything in the World, not just man, when Adam
fell.

In Heaven, God watches the advance of Sin and
Death and remarks to the Son and the angels that he
has permitted them to enter the world so that they can
act as a kind of sanitation system. At Christ's second
coming the mouth of Hell and all its filthy contents
will be sealed up, and Heaven and Earth will be
renewed. But not until then.

God assigns angels to jobs which will make the
world look the way we know it now. These angels
bring about summer and winter; arrange the planets
to bring about bad influences; push the earth several
degrees off a vertical axis; alter the sun's path so that
all parts of the earth have seasonal changes; and cause
the North, South, East and West winds to bring the

extremes of weather which make life difficult. Death begins to affect the animals as Sin's daughter Discord does her work.

Milton is describing the postlapsarian world—the world after the Fall, or "lapse." The contrast with the prelapsarian world makes you feel the enormity of Adam's disobedience.

Lines 715–1104. Adam and Eve in Despair

No one could be feeling worse than Adam feels as he watches these appalling changes ruining his world. His long lament begins with the eternal question "Why was I born?" and continues with "When can I die?" It is a meditation on Death by one who doesn't know what to expect and is thoroughly frightened. But the speech also marks Adam's growth: he accepts the responsibility for what has happened, even though he knows that all mankind will curse him for it. No one except Satan himself can approach the enormity of Adam's crime or the eternal extent of his "doom."

Adam lies writhing in misery on the ground, hoping for the relief of Death which will not come. Eve approaches to comfort him, but he turns on her savagely and calls her "serpent."

The following speech sums up all the fury and venom which men have felt for women through the ages. It includes the famous image of the crooked rib, the symbol of everything dishonest about women. The speech is vibrant with Milton's own personal fury against women. Despite his three marriages—or because of them—Milton felt unable to trust women. Everything goes wrong when a man tries to find "fit mate."

In Milton's case, a wife is first "withheld / By parents," referring to his experience with Mary Powell, whose Royalist family kept her away from Milton for more than three years after they were married. Then he speaks of his experience with Miss Davies, whom he met after he was married and realized she was his "happiest choice" too late. (He does not mention here that he lost his second wife, whom he loved dearly and called his "espoused saint," after only slightly more than a year of marriage.)

Eve takes the only course likely to succeed: she falls at Adam's feet and begs forgiveness. She too finally takes responsibility for her fault, pointing out that she sinned doubly, against Adam and against God. Adam relents. They must work together to lighten their burden now that they must live "A long day's dying."

Eve makes two more suggestions, both of which Adam—now stronger against Eve's arguments by dreadful experience—rejects. She suggests to him that they should not make love so that there will be no children to suffer eternally for their sin. Alternatively, she says, let us kill ourselves now.

Adam has reassumed his leadership in their marriage. Death will not cheat God, for he will find some way to make us feel Death; instead let us live and produce children so that the other part of God's judgment may be performed, the part which promises destruction through the woman's offspring: "to crush his head / Would be revenge indeed."

The idea revives Adam's spirits. Look, Eve, he says, we are still alive—God did not kill us at once. On you he laid the pains of childbirth, but they have their counterpart in the joy of the new baby. I have to work for what we eat, but that is not so bad. Work is better than idleness, and God will help us to cope with the seasons and the weather. He will answer our prayers with fire and other things we need, so that we may live quite comfortably. Let us both go and ask forgiveness on the same spot where he judged us. He will treat us with mercy when we confess our responsibility for our sin.

And so Adam quite unconsciously follows Eve's example: she fell on the ground before him, her God ("he for God only, she for God in him"), and was comforted and forgiven. Now they both do the same, confident in God's grace.

BOOK XI

Lines 1–125. God's Judgment

When Adam and Eve's prayers go up to Heaven, it is the Son who pleads for them. He is beginning to assume his role as man's advocate before God the Father, a role he will complete when he becomes Jesus Christ and is sacrificed for man's sins.

God grants the Son's plea not to kill Adam and Eve at once, but to give them death as a merciful end to an unhappy life. Adam had two gifts: happiness and immortality. Now both are gone.

God calls a meeting of the heavenly host to announce his decision. Look at this speech (lines 84–98) if you are interested in the character of Milton's God and the logic (or lack of it) of his position. Man, he says, has become like us, for now he knows good and evil. He must leave the Garden of Paradise in case he also eats fruit from the Tree of Life and becomes immortal like us.

You might want to consider these questions about God's argument: Is God frightened that Adam will gain more power? Since he is omniscient, doesn't he know whether in the future Adam will eat the fruit of the other tree? God's speech makes us worry again about the relationship between God's foreknowledge and his omnipotence.

Michael—the archangel who wielded the two-handed sword in the War in Heaven—is given the job of escorting Adam and Eve out of Paradise.

Lines 126–208. Hopes and Fears

Praying together has made Adam and Eve feel more lovingly toward each other. They hope they can go on with their work in the garden, and they set out for it. But Adam sees unfavorable signs and expresses his fears to Eve.

NOTE: Omens   The unfavorable signs that frighten Adam are an eclipse, an eagle chasing two brightly colored birds, and a beast (possibly a lion) hunting down a female and a male deer. The three together forecast what is to happen. An eclipse is regarded in religions and myths throughout the world as a sign of Heaven's anger—the withdrawal of light is a drastic step because man depends on light for life. In this case, the eclipse makes a dramatic background for the arrival of Michael and his band of angels, who descend in a white cloud from Heaven.

The eagle and the lion are both animals associated with the highest gods—the eagle is "the bird of Jove." Their victims are clearly symbols of Adam and Eve. So the signs mean that God will drive them out of Paradise.

Milton is following classical tradition when he introduces symbolic signs. The Romans were especially fond of looking for indications of the future in the behavior of birds and animals. The superstition survives in our belief that a black cat crossing in front of you brings you bad luck (if you are an American) or good luck (if you are European).

Lines 208–420. Sentence on Adam and Eve

Adam's misgivings increase as he sees that the angel sent down is not Raphael, who is "sociably mild," but someone much sterner. He tells Eve to leave. She obeys at once.

From her hiding place she hears Michael tell Adam that they are to leave the garden. Her speech sounds like the reaction of any woman who is told she must leave a house where she has been happy. How can we even breathe the air anywhere else?

The archangel Michael tells Eve that she must adapt herself. She must follow her husband: "Where he abides, think there thy native soil."

Adam's sorrow comes from a different source, one more suitable to his direct connection with God. If he is no longer in Paradise, how will he be able to talk with God and his messengers, the angels? Michael assures him that God will be everywhere in the World. He gave all the earth, not merely Paradise, to man to rule, and if all had gone according to the original plan, eventually Adam's offspring would range out from Paradise, which would become a capital city.

In his love, God has sent Michael to show Adam how the world will develop. He makes Eve sleep while Adam sees images of the future—a reversal of the situation when Eve was made out of Adam's rib.

Michael and Adam go up Mount Niphates in order to look down on the earth. An epic comparison tells us that the hill is "not higher" or "wider looking round" than the hill from which Satan tempted Jesus Christ by showing him the whole World. The long string of names impresses with the sense that everything—even the Incas' cities in South America—can be seen from the hill. The comparison has a deeper significance: the temptation of Christ by Satan on the desert mountain is the subject of *Paradise Regained*, a much shorter poem. Milton was obviously thinking about it, because he refers to Christ in this passage as "our second Adam."

Michael treats Adam's eyes with herbs so that he may be better able to see what is in store. But Adam faints from the effects of three drops from the Well of Life and has to be revived.

NOTE: Old and New Testament History   The events of the poem are now basically over, except for the unbearably sad departure from Paradise. If you have seen a tragedy or read one, you know that the final scenes usually bring you out of horror and despair by restoring the sense that life goes on. You are told what happens to the other characters after the main ones are dead. There is a sense of healing and hope for future calm.

The final part of Book XI and all of Book XII have this function in *Paradise Lost*. They constitute a flash-forward to the events related in the Old and New Testaments of the Bible. The narrative takes us up to the Flood by the end of Book XI and continues through the life of Christ and a forecast of the Last Judgment in Book XII.

The Old Testament tells the history of the people in the countries surrounding the Red Sea and the Eastern Mediterranean, the countries we now call Israel,

Egypt, Syria, Jordan, and Lebanon. It is a sacred text in three religions, Judaism, Christianity, and Islam.

The New Testament is a sacred text in Christianity, which believes that Jesus Christ was the Messiah prophesied in the Old Testament. (Jesus is also a prophet in Islam, but he does not have the central status he has in Christianity. Judaism does not believe the Messiah has come yet.) The New Testament also gives us the history of the early Christian church, and it culminates in the Book of Revelation, a mystic vision from which Milton took much of his description of angels, heavenly ceremony, the War in Heaven, and the Last Judgment.

You will come away from a reading of Books XI and XII with a general overview of the main events in both testaments. But there's much more here than a simple summary; Milton gives his opinions on his political and religious enemies and explains Christian doctrine throughout.

Lines 371–551. Death and Old Age

Remember that Adam has no idea what to expect from death. It's just a word to him. When Michael shows him Cain killing Abel, he cries out that "some great mischief" has happened to him. Michael explains that these two are Adam's own sons, so that he is seeing all at once the first death, the first murder, and the first fratricide.

Adam is horrified that death is so ugly and dirty, for Abel rolls "in dust and gore" as he dies. Michael makes him feel even worse as he shows him a hospital with people dying from all manner of diseases, some of them even crying for death as a release.

Adam's distress brings from Michael the explanation that the sin of Eve brought down on mankind the curse of sickness because she did not respect God's image in herself. Sickness comes from excesses which pervert the image of God in every person.

However, Michael says to comfort Adam, if you live temperately, you will die of old age, not sickness. He gives a touchingly realistic picture of old age, with its lost youth, strength, and beauty and its "melancholy damp of cold and dry." The result is that Adam thinks death a deliverance from "this cumbrous charge," life, which he isn't so eager now to prolong. Michael sums up the discussion in a two-line moral:

> Nor love thy life nor hate; but what thou livst
> Live well, how long or short permit to Heaven.

Lines 556–898. Noah and the Flood

Michael shows to Adam the sons of Cain corrupted by "fair atheists," prompting a bitter response from Adam: men's troubles always begin with women. Michael immediately rebukes him: you can't blame women—blame your own "effeminate slackness." Man has superior gifts and should use them.

Things get worse as the children of those "ill-fated marriages" first fight among themselves and then give themselves up to riotous self-indulgence. Only one man, Noah, tries to stop them. He doesn't get anywhere, so he moves away and then builds an ark. He knows what God is going to do.

Adam is in despair again as he sees the entire earth swallowed up in the flood, with only Noah and the creatures in his ark saved. He tells Michael that he isn't enjoying seeing what is to come: no one should see what will happen to his "seed," his descendants, because he can't do anything to change it and can only suffer.

But it gives Michael a chance to praise Noah, and this gives Milton a chance to talk about himself. As you will remember from the invocation to Book VII, Milton felt himself the only defender of truth left when the Royalists returned. He was

> the only son of light
> In a dark age, against example good
> Against allurement, custom, and a world
> Offended . . .

Like Noah, he dares to stand up for what is right when everyone else is wrong.

As Michael tells the rest of the story of Noah and the ark, he shows that the Mount of Paradise will be moved by the force of the water from Mesopotamia down through the Persian Gulf to become an island. By including this detail, Milton was able to do justice to two traditions—one which said Paradise was between the Tigris and the Euphrates, and one which said it was one of the South seas islands.

Adam is relieved to see that mankind gets a sign from God, the rainbow, as a pledge that he won't drown the world again.

BOOK XII

Lines 1–360. The History of the Children of Israel

The history rolls on, through the story of the Tower of Babel; Abraham, Joseph, and the journey to Egypt; the freeing of the Israelites by Moses, with the parting of the Red Sea; the Ten Commandments given to Moses by God; and the making of the Holy Tabernacle.

When the narrative gets to Joshua, Adam interrupts to ask why mankind needs so many laws, for "so many laws argue so many sins." This gives Michael (who is clearly the voice of Milton) an opportunity to say that laws discover sin because they provoke the sinful to break them, which of course brings on more laws. But law can't remove sin. Law shows a need to make recompense for sin; it accustoms man to the need for internal discipline. Milton thinks law is inferior to faith, the free acceptance of God's will.

After Joshua (whose name is close to that of Jesus—both mean "savior") has brought the Israelites into the promised land of Canaan, they continue to have political troubles, including their seventy-year captivity in Babylon. In fact, they are so politically messed up that when their Messiah, Jesus Christ, the Son of God in human form, arrives, the Jews are ruled by the Romans.

Lines 360–480. God the Son Becomes Man

The story of Christ's birth is told in lines 360–371. You might also want to read Milton's earlier poem, "Hymn on the Morning of Christ's Nativity," which is a wonderful musical celebration of the virgin birth.

The news brings great joy to Adam, who is able at last to see something good coming from the "seed" of Eve. At last, he thinks, his descendants will bruise the serpent's head.

NOTE: The Doctrine of the "Felix Culpa," the "Happy Fault"   In Christian doctrine, Adam's sin is looked on not only as the origin of all pain, death, and sin in the world, but also—paradoxically—as the source of all our joy. Because Adam sinned, God sent his Son down to become the man Jesus Christ and save the world. If Adam had not sinned, there would be no savior. So his was a "happy fault," "felix culpa" in Latin, sometimes also translated as the "fortunate fall."

The crucifixion and death of Christ fulfill the prophesy that Eve's seed shall bruise the heel of Satan. Man's sins are atoned for. Christ will return to Heaven after his resurrection—when he defeats Death—and there will wait until his Second Coming. Then he will return to judge the entire world, and man will join the angels in Heaven.

The news of this eventual reconciliation with God causes Adam to break out in a hymn of praise to God. He wonders whether he should repent of his sin or rejoice that the "felix culpa" will bring about such a triumphant ending for mankind.

Lines 480–551. The Holy Spirit and the Christian Church

In answer to Adam's question as to who will guide the people after Christ goes back to Heaven, Michael describes the coming of the Holy Ghost, or Holy Spirit. You will remember from the note to Book III that the Christian God is a trinity, but the Holy Spirit is not mentioned until men need him. Like the Father and the Son, he has been present from the beginning. It is the Holy Spirit to whom Milton prays for help with writing *Paradise Lost*, as you will remember from the very first lines.

The future history of the church isn't all smooth sailing, however. The "wolves" referred to in line 508 are the popes of the Roman Catholic Church, whom Milton saw as deceivers, using the church to make themselves wealthy. (In his time he was probably justified; think about the magnificent buildings full of statues and paintings built by the Renaissance popes and their families.)

The world will go on in the same way, the good suffering and the bad prospering, until the Day of Judgment, when all shall get what they deserve and "new heavens and new earth" will be "founded in righteousness and peace and love."

Lines 551–649. The Final Walk Through Paradise

Milton has poured all the Christian wisdom necessary for a good life into Adam's final speech. Adam has learned the hard way, but now he knows that to obey is best, that dependence on God's truth will bring him mercy and strength. It must be Milton's own voice we hear in the lines: "That suffering for Truth's sake / Is fortitude to highest victory."

Michael sees that he's finished his work, for Adam has "attained the sum / Of wisdom." He urges him to live in faith, virtue, patience, temperance, but to add love to all of these. If he takes love with him in his soul, he will not be leaving Paradise but will have it always with him.

The time has come to leave the Garden. Adam has 930 more years to live on earth with Eve, but they will be strengthened and comforted by the knowledge of the redeemer who is to arise from their "seed."

Eve already knows everything through her dream. What Milton is saying here is that women have a more direct access to some kinds of knowledge through their intuition. Eve also rejoices in her "felix culpa": "though all by me is lost . . . By me the promised seed shall all restore."

Now the archangels glide toward them like a mist rising from the river. This final epic simile of the poem has the usual extra message—the mist seems to urge the laborers home, just as now the angels have to make Adam and Eve hurry. Michael seizes a hand each of Adam and Eve and ushers them through the gate and down to the plain below. He leaves immediately.

Imagine Adam and Eve at this final moment: they look back up at the cliff, their eyes full of tears, and see the gate closed against them. Above it flames the burning sword, and all around are the armed angels with forbidding faces.

They turn away from the cliff and look out to a land they have never seen. It is frightening, but they seek each other's hands and feel strengthened by their trust in God.

These last few lines are not in the Biblical source, as you can see. They express in simple words (look how many are monosyllables) that frightening sense of intense aloneness you feel when beginning a new part of your life. Even though you know that eventually everything will turn out well, those first few steps are hard to take. Like Adam and Eve, we all have to take them.

A STEP BEYOND

Tests and Answers

TESTS

Test 1

1. During the English Civil War, John Milton _____
   was a
   A. religious pacifist
   B. Royalist pamphleteer
   C. Puritan rebel

2. *Paradise Lost* is based on the literary traditions _____
   of
      I. the classical epic
      II. Puritan allegory
      III. the Bible
   A. I and II
   B. II and III
   C. I and III

3. We first meet Satan _____
   A. the day he is thrown out of Heaven
   B. nine days after the War in Heaven
   C. three days after he arrives in Eden

4. One of Satan's fallen angels in Hell is called _____
   A. Abdiel
   B. Uriel
   C. Belial

5. Satan volunteers to go up to earth because _____
   A. the other fallen angels are too cowardly
   B. he wants the glory of revenging himself on God
   C. it's a quick way to escape from Hell

6. The gatekeepers of Hell are _____
   A. Sin and Death
   B. Love and Hate
   C. Chaos and Old Night

7. In Book III, Milton invokes light because _____
   A. he himself was blind
   B. his theme is the light of man's reason
   C. his muse comes from Heaven

8. Adam eats the apple because _____
   A. Satan fools him
   B. he loves Eve
   C. Michael predicts that Christ will redeem mankind

9. After Satan returns to Hell, the fallen angels _____ turn into
   A. dead leaves
   B. snakes
   C. apples that taste like ashes

10. Adam and Eve are led out of Paradise by _____
    A. Satan
    B. Raphael
    C. Michael

11. In Book XII, lines 557–573, Adam speaks of what he has learned. Relate each item to the experience in the poem which is the source of Adam's hard-won wisdom. Are there things that Adam says he has learned which have no clear connection to his experiences?

12. Is Satan the hero or the villain of *Paradise Lost?*

13. The poet William Blake wrote: "The reason Milton wrote in fetters when he wrote of Angels and God, and at liberty when of Devils and Hell, is because he was a true poet and therefore of the devil's party without knowing it." Presumably this means that Milton wrote about the fallen angels and Satan more freely and sympathetically than he did about the other characters. What do you think?

14. Someone who doesn't have much time wants to read the essential parts of *Paradise Lost.* This person has asked you to recommend the six books she ought to read. Name those six books and justify your choice.

15. What are the functions of the epic similes?

Test 2

1. Milton was Latin secretary to   _____
   A. Elizabeth I
   B. Oliver Cromwell
   C. Charles II

2. Milton borrowed these devices from the   _____
   classical epic
      I. an invocation
      II. extended similes
      III. catalogs
      IV. beginning in medias res
   A. I, III, and IV
   B. II and IV only
   C. I, II, III, and IV

3. As Satan addresses his followers in Hell, we   _____
   see that he is
   A. a brilliant leader
   B. ashamed to be in Hell
   C. trying to get back into God's good graces

4. The word "pandemonium" originally meant   _____
   A. a great noise
   B. a house for all devils
   C. a beehive

5. The rebel angel whose mind is on money is   _____
   A. Beelzebub
   B. Mammon
   C. Moloch

6. In a parallel with Satan, Christ volunteers to   _____
   A. become man's savior
   B. lead the loyal angels
   C. explain the ways of God to man

7. The World hangs in the middle of   _____
   A. Heaven
   B. Chaos
   C. Limbo

8. Eve tells Adam he should let her work alone   _____
   because
   A. she is the weaker of the two
   B. Satan told her to do so in a dream
   C. they have a lot of work to get done

9. Satan masquerades as   _____
   A. a cherub
   B. a toad
   C. both of the above

10. Only after the Fall is man made for   _____
    I. death
    II. sex
    III. hard work
    A. I and II only
    B. II and III only
    C. I and III only

11. Eve has two dreams in the poem; there are two great
    councils, one in Heaven and one in Hell; Adam and Eve
    make love twice in the poem. Look carefully at these
    pairs and any others you can find and discuss their
    function.

12. Explain how the structure of the poem helps to tell the
    story.

13. Contrast Adam and Eve's marriage before and after the
    Fall.

14. Discuss free will and freedom in *Paradise Lost*.

15. Show how ordinary logical reason misleads those who
    trust it in the poem.

ANSWERS

Test 1

1. C   **2.** C   **3.** B   **4.** C   **5.** B   **6.** A

7. A   **8.** B   **9.** B   **10.** C

11. Look carefully at the lines in Book XII and separate the things that Adam has learned: it was foolish to seek more knowledge than God allows; he must obey; he must love and fear God; and so on. Then match up each item with the events that brought it home to Adam. For example, he learned from the Fall that God punished his desire for more knowledge than a man should have—a desire expressed symbolically by the eating of the apple from the Tree of Knowledge. But exactly what taught him that he should depend on God alone? Was it the Fall or the merciful way that God treated him? Or was it the visions of the future shown him by Michael? He says that he has learned to suffer for truth's sake, but there isn't any obvious event which teaches him this. You have to ask yourself why Adam says this.

12. Attack this question by asking what makes a hero or a villain. Get a working definition of each, then match Satan's actions and speeches with it. You might think of a hero in a purely formal way as the chief focus of the action: Satan sets everything in motion and makes everyone react to him. There wouldn't be any story if Satan hadn't decided to object to God's elevation of the Son. So in that sense Satan is a hero.

    We also think of heroes as having exemplary characteristics. Does Satan have any? Look at Books I and II, where he rallies the fallen angels and demonstrates leadership qualities. But how did the situation arise that Satan has to demonstrate those qualities? Was his action heroic in the sense of admirable? Can rebellion ever be admirable? Here you can refer to Abdiel—a rebel against a rebel and one with truly heroic qualities.

Villains are easier to deal with than heroes because we use the word "villain" in a more restricted sense. The problem is that villains aren't usually central characters—and Satan is the central character of *Paradise Lost*, isn't he?

13. You need to consider why the fallen angels might be more interesting than God and the angels who remain in Heaven. Why would a poet—a writer—find it easier to make evil more interesting than good? Do you think he did this? Compare Books I and II with Book III. Is the landscape in Hell more interesting than that in Heaven? Where is there more action? Is there argument in one place and not in the other? It seems to be true that we find conflict and action more interesting than unrelieved harmony and peace, so it may be nothing to do with Milton's intentions that we enjoy the scenes in Hell more than those in Heaven.

   There's another dimension to Blake's remark. Quite apart from the artistic problems of making goodness interesting (and the poem contains many examples of interesting evil and boring good), Blake is suggesting that artists—poets—are by nature rebels against authority. Is that the source of Satan's vitality? If you argue that it is, you'll have to consider what to say about the fact that Milton clearly identifies with other people, not with Satan. For proof, look at the invocations and at the comments on Noah in Book XI. This is a topic that has been provoking discussion for over 150 years.

14. Look at each book and summarize briefly its theme and its function in the poem. For example, why is Book VIII there? What information do we get from Adam's

description of the making of Eve? When you think
about what happens in Book IX, you'll see that the
information in Book VIII is essential to the understanding not so much of the Fall but of the conversation
between Adam and Eve before they separate. Then
move a step backward: why Book VII? Is it superfluous?
Could you tell your friend to skip it and make do with a
synopsis? Wouldn't she be missing some of the most
delightful poetry in the whole of *Paradise Lost?* This
book also has a none-too-obvious function: it shows
that the world really is God's idea and that he has a
deep love for it. So this book makes you think differently about God's character. Proceeding in this way, you
may well decide to argue that no book can be omitted if
someone really wants to understand *Paradise Lost.*

15. Let's consider the simile in which the fallen angels are
compared to the fairies a peasant might see on his way
home *(I, 781–789)*. The message is clearly that the fallen
angels have become very small so that they can enter
Pandemonium. The equation is: devils shrunk down to
enter Pandemonium = elves seen by late, possibly
drunken peasants. Why peasants? What is like and
unlike about the two halves of the comparison? What is
in the scene of the fairies and the peasant under the
moon which gives us more information about the devils
and/or our relationship to them? A proper analysis of
the simile will consider each question in turn.

Peasants: Milton frequently chooses country people
for his similes, perhaps to make the unfamiliar seem
familiar, but also to bring in unsophisticated people,
because we are all unsophisticated in relation to the
superhuman powers in *Paradise Lost.*

Like and unlike: The devils are small, and so are the
fairies. They're threatening and mysterious, and so are

the fairies, who inspire the peasant with "joy and fear." Both fairies and devils may or may not be real: "sees, / Or dreams he sees." The fairies are having a party ("midnight revels"), but the devils are intent on very grim business in Pandemonium.

Other information: The fairies and the peasant meet each other at nght, under a huge moon. This makes us think that Hell must look like that too, dark and full of shadows. Thus we get this information without being told it directly. When the moon, who according to astrology has influence over our destinies, moves closer to the earth, it makes us feel uneasy. And we certainly ought to feel uneasy when the devils meet! The peasant feels confused, not sure what's going on or what he sees, excited by the music but frightened by seeing what he thinks are supernatural beings. We feel confused by the devils; they have their attractive side, but in fact they are deadly threats.

As you analyze similes in this way, you'll realize that each has its own function or functions, in addition to indicating that Milton is writing in the epic tradition.

Test 2

1. B   **2.** C   **3.** A   **4.** B   **5.** B   **6.** A

7. B   **8.** C   **9.** C   **10.** C

11. Milton has deliberately taken one action and described it in two contexts. What is he saying in each version? Consider Eve's two dreams: who causes the dream in Book V? Who causes the dream in Books XI and XII? What happens in each? Are both prophetic? (in the same sense?) What should Eve have learned from each? Did she learn? What feelings are generated from each dream—for Eve and for you, the reader? You will need to ask and then answer questions like these for each of the pairs in order to go beyond the most obvious conclusion, that Milton wanted to show how one thing—a dream, a council, lovemaking—is different under the influence of Heaven and under the influence of Hell.

12. Think about how the poem moves from Hell to Heaven, then to earth, then through four books of flashbacks, then to the climactic action, and then through three books of consequences. Does this remind you of a play? a movie? a serial? anything else? What does starting in Hell do for the focus? It certainly tends to make Satan extraordinarily important, and it makes it more difficult for us to find God sympathetic.

    What do those flashbacks do? You might think about a TV movie you've seen or some other dramatic presentation in which flashbacks are important. Writers use flashbacks because they want to interest you in the story before they give you information you might not find fascinating until you care about what's going on. Is this what Milton did?

    The climax of *Paradise Lost* is clearly Book IX, but we wouldn't understand the significance of the events in it without the long buildup. Then there are still three

books to go. The note on Book XI in the Story section
tells something about the function of Books XI and XII,
and you should be able to think of other reasons why
they are essential to the story and the meaning.

13. Look first at descriptions of Adam and Eve before the
Fall. Book IV covers almost a complete day, and Book V
describes the wakening and morning activities. You will
have to decide how much of Book IX can be thought of
as before the Fall, for Eve is behaving a little differently
under the influence of her dream. You'll want to talk
about Adam's description of the formation of Eve and
his passionate love for her. The big question is: was the
marriage ideal before the Fall, or were there the seeds of
problems?

   Look then at what happens right after Eve has eaten
the apple; Adam's decision to follow Eve into destruction has its roots in their relationship. Consider their
actions in the rest of Book IX and how their relationship
slowly begins to heal in Book X. In Books XI and XII it
has stabilized. How do Adam and Eve put up with their
punishments, including their expulsion from Paradise?
Is the marriage the same as it was in Book IV? Has it
deteriorated or gotten better? Has it moved closer to the
ideal, "he for God only, she for God in him?"

14. God's discussion of free will in Book III is the central
statement in the poem about free will and determinism.
In Milton's philosophy, you experience free will and
can exercise it, even though God knows what is to happen. Criticize this notion if you want to, but understand
that it is the framework of the poem's action.

   You'll want to consider the nature of true freedom
and false freedom, contrasting those characters who
know what true freedom is and accept it, and those
who follow their own concept of freedom and suffer the

consequences. Abdiel is probably the best example of a character who understands true freedom, the acceptance of God's will and perfect obedience. Notice how God praises him. Satan, Eve, and then Adam follow their own will, and paradoxically they end up in servitude—the opposite of freedom.

There are even more interesting questions to explore. How free is God? There are significant actions God can't take, such as destroying Satan. And apparently he can't alter the plan set out for the Fall. Is he then free? At the end he leaves Satan alone in Hell, and Satan seems to be free to go on causing trouble for the World. He doesn't even remain a serpent for long. The question of freedom isn't a simple one.

Try to relate this to your own experience. Are you really free to do exactly what you want? How is your freedom limited? Do you trust any exterior force, such as God? Perhaps we all do, in the sense that we have to trust what we're given as mental and physical equipment. Thinking about your own ideas will help you to understand the choices made by the poem's characters.

15. Make a list of speeches that rely on logic, and you'll have a nice lot of examples to choose from. First there are the speeches of Moloch, Belial, Mammon, Beelzebub, and Satan in Book II, all of which are perfectly logical. You'll begin to realize that logical doesn't mean correct from the fact that several of the speeches contradict each other. Then look at Satan's argument with Abdiel; Adam's arguments to God when he wants a mate; Adam and Eve's dispute on the morning of the Fall; the serpent's arguments to Eve; Eve's arguments to herself when she decides to drag Adam down with her; and Adam and Eve's quarrels after the Fall.

(As part of your answer, you'll need to contrast these speeches with others that don't rely on logic. You might refer to Adam's speech summing up his wisdom in Book XII and to several of Michael's pieces of advice to Adam.)

Consider the logical structure of one or two of the speeches. Ask what are the premises (assumptions) of the argument, and what do the speakers think is implied by those premises. For example, Eve is deceived by the serpent's argument that he has eaten the fruit and he isn't dead, so why should she die?

In the end you should be able to make statements about the importance of assumptions to reasonable arguments and about the difference between trusting to logic and trusting in God's will. If Eve had distrusted her own logic and trusted God's commands, she would not have believed the serpent.

Term Paper Ideas

The Characters

1. Show how Satan changes from the beginning of the poem to the end.

2. Show how Adam changes from the beginning of the poem to the end.

3. Show the changes in Eve's character throughout the poem.

4. Contrast Raphael and Michael.

5. Look at the speeches of Moloch, Belial, and Mammon and describe their characters from those speeches.

6. Contrast Moloch, Belial, and Mammon with Sin and Death, showing how allegorical figures differ from characters.

7. Consider the characteristics of angels, using Gabriel, Abdiel, Raphael, Michael, and Uriel as examples.

8. Contrast Satan and the Son, especially in their relationship to God.

9. Choose an angel and a devil (one of the fallen angels) and compare them as examples of angels and devils in general.

10. Is God the ideal parent?

11. Contrast Satan and Abdiel.

12. Look at the dialog between Adam and Eve in Book IX, when Eve suggests working separately from Adam. What do their speeches tell us about their characters at this point?

13. Choose your favorite character in *Paradise Lost* and explain why you find this character attractive.

The Events

1. Describe exactly what happens at the debate in Pandemonium. Who speaks? What decisions are made? Who makes them? What do we learn about the devils, individually and collectively, from this debate?

2. Describe Satan's journey from the time he leaves Hell until the time he returns. Why does he go where he goes?

3. Count carefully how many visitors from Heaven come down to see Adam and Eve. Briefly describe the purpose of each visit.

4. Tell the life story of Sin and Death. Why are they in the poem?

5. Contrast life in Hell and in Heaven, especially as you see it described in Book II and Book III.

6. What happens in a normal day in Paradise before the Fall? How would you characterize the life Adam and Eve live?

7. Look at the incidents in Book IX leading up to the Fall. Write a blow-by-blow description of exactly how Eve is seduced by the serpent. Is one factor more important than others for the outcome?

8. What happens to everything else in the World after the Fall? Consider what we are told about the animals, plants, weather, seasons, and planets.

The Meaning

1. Compare the Biblical story of creation and the version told in Book VII and explain the differences. (Consider only the creation story, as in Chapter 1 and the beginning of Chapter 2 of Genesis, not the Fall.)

2. Dr. Johnson said: "Epic poetry undertakes to teach the most important truths by the most pleasing precepts, and therefore relates some great event in the most affecting manner." Does *Paradise Lost* fulfill this definition of epic?

3. Who does Satan deceive most?

4. The fruit that God forbids Adam and Eve to eat comes from the Tree of Knowledge. Can you justify this in any way? Is there some knowledge man ought not to have?

5. Why does Milton use the schematic Ptolemaic universe as a background to his poem instead of the Copernican one he clearly knew? How does it fit with the events and the message of the poem?

6. Discuss the events of Book X as consequences of the Fall. Interpret their meaning.

7. Why is the atmosphere of Hell so elaborately described in Books I and II? Discuss what this introduction does for the meaning of the poem.

8. Unless you are a fundamentalist Christian, you can't take the story of *Paradise Lost* literally. But taken as a myth, does it have any meaning for you at the end of the twentieth century?

9. Is it necessary to the meaning of the poem for God to be distant, even unpleasantly forbidding?

Further Reading

BIOGRAPHY

Wilson, A. N. *The Life of John Milton*. Oxford: Oxford University Press, 1983.

CRITICAL WORKS

Broadbent, John. *Paradise Lost: Introduction*. Cambridge: Cambridge University Press, 1972.

Fish, Stanley E. *Surprised by Sin*. Berkeley: University of California Press, 1971.

Gardner, Helen. *A Reading of Paradise Lost*. Oxford: Oxford University Press, 1965.

Johnson, Samuel. "Milton" in *The Lives of the Poets*. 1779.

Lewis, C. S. *A Preface to Paradise Lost*. Oxford: Oxford University Press, 1942.

AUTHOR'S OTHER WORKS

"L'Allegro" and "Il Penseroso"   Two enchanting lyrical poems celebrating the active and the contemplative life.

"Hymn on the Morning of Christ's Nativity"   A magnificent celebration of Christ's birth in musical verse.

"Sonnet on his blindness"   A poem of resignation, ending in the famous line "They also serve who only stand and wait."

"Lycidas"   A lyric poem mourning for a drowned friend.

Samson Agonistes   Written after *Paradise Lost*, a Greek drama on the Biblical story of Samson, the blind hero who pulled down the temple on the assembled Philistines.

Glossary

This glossary does not include all the words that Milton uses in senses different from the senses in which we use them now. If it did, it would be a good deal longer than this entire book. Most of those words will be explained in footnotes in your edition of *Paradise Lost*, or you will find them in a good dictionary. What you will find here are names and terms which are used often throughout the poem and aren't necessarily found in a regular dictionary.

Adam The first man, placed in Paradise by God. He asked for a mate, so God made Eve from his rib.

Angels The servants of God. The word comes from the Greek word "angellos," which means a messenger. The angels were created next to God in the universal hierarchy, above man.

Archangels The highest order of angels, those entrusted with God's most important business. Gabriel, Michael, Uriel, and Raphael are among the archangels we meet.

Argument The subject matter of the poem or the speech (not a verbal dispute).

Beelzebub A fallen angel, second-in-command to Satan.

Belial A fallen angel who speaks in the debate in Pandemonium.

Chaos The primal stuff which fills all the space between Hell, Heaven, and the World. Chaos is both the name of the space-filling material and the name of the ruler of Chaos. God takes pieces of Chaos to make Hell and the World.

Cherub A young angel. The plural is cherubim, a Hebrew form.

Eden The land in Mesopotamia, between the rivers Tigris and Euphrates, where the Garden of Paradise is situated.

Eve The "mother of mankind," the first woman, made from Adam's rib and given to him as a mate in the Garden of Paradise.

Fall The name given to Adam and Eve's disobedience. It is also called original sin.

Fallen Angels The followers of Satan who were pushed out of Heaven on the third day of the war and must live in Hell.

Free Will The subjective sense that angels and men have that they can choose all their actions, even though God knows the outcome in advance.

Gabriel The archangel who guards Paradise. He was second-in-command to Michael in the War in Heaven.

Gate of Heaven The place at the top of the World (the universe) where there is a stairway going up to Heaven, an opening to go down into the ten concentric circles which make up the World, and the end of a road from Hell.

Gate of Hell Sin and Death stand guard here; after Sin opens the gate for Satan, it can never be closed again.

God He has three aspects: the Father, the Son, and the Holy Spirit. In *Paradise Lost*, God means the Father. God is creator of all things, omnipotent and omniscient, with foreknowledge of all that is to happen.

Hell Located directly opposite to Heaven, this is where Satan and his followers are sent after they lose the War in Heaven.

Limbo A place where souls go who belong neither in Hell nor in Heaven, it lies on the outside rim of the World.

Mammon A fallen angel who loves gold.

Michael The archangel who escorts Adam and Eve out of Paradise.

Moloch A belligerent fallen angel.

Pandemonium The hall built by Mulciber and Mammon in Hell for the great debate among the fallen angels.

Paradise   The garden in Eden which God has given Adam and Eve to live in and from which they are expelled after the Fall.

Raphael   The angel who tells Adam the story of the War in Heaven and the creation.

Seraphim   Hebrew plural, meaning angels.

Uriel   The angel who guards the sun.

World   In *Paradise Lost*, the universe. It consists of ten concentric circles with earth at the center (see diagram, page 28).

The Critics

I am, however, of opinion, that no just Heroic Poem ever was or can be made, from whence one great Moral may be deduced. That which reigns in Milton, is the most universal and most useful that can be imagined: It is in short this, That Obedience to the Will of God makes Men happy, and that Disobedience makes them miserable. This is visibly the Moral of the principal Fable, which turns upon Adam and Eve, who continued in Paradise, while they kept the Command that was given them, and were driven out of it as soon as they transgressed. This is likewise the Moral of the principal episode, which shews us how an innumerable Multitude of Angels fell from their State of Bliss, and were cast into Hell upon their Disobedience.

> *Joseph Addison and Richard Steele*, The Spectator, *3 May 1712*

He was naturally a thinker for himself, confident of his own abilities, and disdainful of help or hindrance: he did not refuse admission to the thought or images of his predecessors, but he did not seek them. . . . His great works were performed under discountenance, and in blindness, but difficulties vanished at his touch; he was born for whatever is arduous; and his work is not the greatest of heroick poems, only because it is not the first.

> *Samuel Johnson, "Milton" in* Lives of the Poets, *1779*

Milton's chief ethical interest was freedom. He wanted to be free of his own appetites, and the appetites of others, especially tyranny. Repeatedly he says you can't have the second freedom without the first; and since the fall that is difficult.

> *John Broadbent*, Paradise Lost: Introduction, *1972, page 75*

The epic poet does not write to convince doubters or to propagate individual views, but to "assert." It is, of course, just those matters which an age assumes to be beyond questioning that later ages question, and epic poetry demands therefore a greater effort of imagination and a greater willingness to grant the writer's premises than does drama or lyric poetry. The poetic greatness of *Paradise Lost* is in large measure due to the fact that Milton was able to take so much for granted. He was not writing a work of Christian apologetics on the one hand or a symbolic novel on the other. He was writing an epic poem, retelling the best-known story in the world, and a story whose main meaning and import he did not have to establish.

Helen Gardner, A Reading of
Paradise Lost, *1965, page 15*

We are never, for one moment, away from Milton in *Paradise Lost*. It is overwhelmingly the product of his mind and his genius. But the vocation to "assert eternal providence" is faithfully pursued. His darkened eyes search out "thrones, dominations, princedoms, virtues, powers." And it is from the Archangel that Adam receives the reassurance that though He is now invisible, God's presence follows his people through the world. The vision must be *asserted* because it will never, in the realm of nature, be automatically *felt*.

A. N. Wilson, The Life of John
Milton, *1983, page 213*

Printed in the United States
6252

9 780764 191206